The Dark Wizard of Oz

THE DARK WIZARD OF OZ
SEX, DRUGS, AND THE LARGEST BREACH
OF BANK SECURITY IN U.S. HISTORY

MICHAEL TAROMINA
WITH OZZY LEMBO

OVER THE EDGE BOOKS

Los Angeles

Title fonts by MrSuma, DarkX ShadowX21

Some names and identifying details have been changed
to protect the privacy of individuals.

Published by Over the Edge Books, Los Angeles, overtheedgebooks.com

Printed in the United States of America

ISBN-13 978-0996423809 (electronic formats)
ISBN-13 978-0996423816 (print)

10 9 8 7 6 5 4 3 2 1

For Orazio Sr., Antonette, and Joe Lembo

Le persone piú oneste che conosco.

Please allow me to introduce myself...

ONE

*R**ING!*

ING!

"HELLO," AN OLDER WOMAN ANSWERS. She's not my target. A normal bill collector would hang up and try again later, but that's not me.

My lying commences with, "Ma'am, my name is Detective Magna. I'm the chief investigator for the Paterson Police Department Financial Fraud Unit and I am trying to reach a Mr. Leroy Farrow. Is he there with you?"

"Leroy is unavailable," she replies curtly. "This is his mother." *Excellent! His mother.* This could be better than I originally hoped for.

"Mrs. Farrow, I'm calling regarding a warrant for your son's arrest."

"Well, like I said, he is not here." She is getting a bit chilly toward me. This means she believes my bullshit.

"Okay, Mrs. Farrow. Do you know when your son will be back?"

"I have no idea." She's being downright cold. Exactly what I want.

"Mrs. Farrow, as a courtesy, I'm going to leave you the name and telephone number of the individual that filed the warrant. If your son wants to, he can contact the complainant directly and see if his arrest can be avoided. Please be advised that after 24 hours, if this matter has not been formally dropped by the complainant, then my unit will execute on the warrant. Do you understand?" Everything I just told her is untrue.

"Yes, I do. Please Detective, give me a moment to get a pen and paper."

"Take your time, Mrs. Farrow." I have a bong hit to do anyway. *Inhale.*

Exhale, and she's back. "Go ahead, Detective."

I provide her the name of my alias, Mr. Michael Hart, a bogus warrant number, and a valid telephone number—to a completely different line within the same office I'm talking to her from.

"I got it. Thank you, Officer," she says and hangs up.

I made thousands of calls like this and this was the first time that a mother had no interest in as to *why* I was planning on arresting her son. I must admit Mamma Farrow had me quite curious. If you tried calling my mother and saying something like I just did, you'd hear a verbal machine gun of 30 questions you could not understand fired off within the next two minutes. By the time my mother was done babbling incoherently, you were likely to just pretend it's the wrong number and hang up.

A few moments pass and then, "Hart! You got a Mrs. Farrow on line four," shouts my secretary.

"Michael Hart, may I help you?" My voice is suddenly twenty years older.

"Hello there, Mr. Hart. This is Mrs. Farrow and I'm calling regarding my son Leroy. A police officer just called about some kind of warrant for his arrest. Can you please tell me what it is regarding?" *Well, well, well. Mamma Farrow is curious, after all.*

"Yes, I can. Did the officer give you a warrant number?"

"He did. It's DC-083171-93."

I repeat back to her the numbers slowly like I'm checking them against my paperwork though I am actually loading my bong again.

"That's correct," she confirms.

"Please hold while I get the file." I place her on hold and look at the bad check in the file I have on my desk for Leroy Farrow. It is for $140 and was written to a local Shop Rite. I pick the phone back up.

"Okay, I have the file here, Mrs. Farrow. It's a series of bad checks written to our client Shop Rite in Wayne, New Jersey. We sent your son multiple civil notifications of the complaint to 120 Park Avenue in Paterson, New Jersey, and he never responded. Suit was filed and, because the claim is criminal in nature, an arrest warrant has now been issued."

"He didn't respond because he's been in rehab for over a month. He is not scheduled to be released for another 60 days so I would like to take care of this for him." Wow. It appears Mamma Farrow has clearly been through the wringer with her son. I definitely could relate to her plight. After all, I tortured my loving mother my entire life. This is the point in the conversation where a human being with a soul, especially a compassionate and remorseful son who easily relates to a poor mother's plight, would reconsider what he's attempting to do.

"Please hold for the total," I say.

After another bong hit, I add the one original check, plus the fake ones I made up. Plus this. Plus that. Plus my time, my energy, and the cost of my inevitable one-way ticket to hell. I pick the phone back up and tell her the bad news, "It comes out to $1,822.45."

The next morning, Mamma Farrow comes to my office—I mean Michael Hart's office—to hand us a cashier's check for the amount I told her. I don't come out to meet her. That would have been cruel. Besides, I was busy booking my high-speed train ticket to hell.

Eventually, my high-speed rail ride to damnation was traded in for a rocket ship. It ended with my arrest that landed on the front cover of newspapers around the world. After all, 1.6 trillion dollars was larger than the GDP of most countries. My crimes shocked common sense. It shocked people's conscious. It shocked me with how wrong the government's figures were. The truth was my career totals were much higher than they calculated.

The media swarmed in wanting a picture or sound bite from this diabolical, shadowy financial wizard. Most of all, they wanted to know how the hell I did it. And how the hell I got away with it for so many years.

They knew I didn't use a weapon so experts immediately assumed I hacked my way in. People were convinced I was some evil computer genius in a deep, dark underground cave typing away—surgically piercing the most sophisticated security systems in the world with my fingertips. The truth was I took a couple Intro to Computer classes in high school but could not concentrate on most of the training because some of the hottest girls in my school took the same classes. Instead, I used my doctorate in street studies and silver tongue to shock the financial world. It sounded too impossible for people to grasp at the time.

Probably still does today. How could one person *talk* their way into banks and other protected places and *talk* their way back out with stolen goods without a trace?

The only people who would believe that was possible were people that heard me talk.

✦ ✖ ✦

Growing up in northern New Jersey, I was introduced to illegal collections at an early age. By the time I was a teenager, I was already collecting debts for local mob bosses, bookies, and loan sharks. Before that, I was the second and last-born boy to Italian immigrant parents in 1970. They gave me a common American name, Orazio. I'm still surprised to see Orazio has not caught on in the New World. But Ozzy was easier to say and proved to be more appropriate, especially after Mr. Osbourne bit the head off a bat. I certainly did my best in life to live up to the Prince of Darkness's *high* standards. I think he would be proud. And probably jealous.

From childhood, I was different from the other kids, most notably during lunch. While they carried Scooby-Doo lunchboxes containing peanut butter and jelly sandwiches to school, I hauled a large brown bag from Corrado's Italian Market that had a feast for a small family inside. Sometimes it was ravioli in meat sauce with sausage on the side or cavatelli pasta with garlic, olive oil, and broccoli rabe. Yes, we are talking about a school lunch here. Often it included prosciutto, mortadella, capicola, salami, and soppresseta.[1]

Then there was dessert, which was always a half-frozen treat. Italian parents freeze everything. I mean *everything*. My parents had a double coffin-sized freezer in our basement where they kept everything except Walt Disney. The Iceman killer, I heard, had the only other model. Inside my mother's ice tomb was a frozen tundra containing every kind of food from apples to Snapples. In case of a nuclear holocaust, the Lembos were just a defrosting away from feeding our whole town for a week. One year, I persuaded my guidance counselor into switching my lunch period from fourth to sixth so that my cannolis had an additional eighty minutes to thaw out properly. Fortunately, he understood the value of biting into a cannoli at just the right temperature. *Buono!*

The best part about being raised in an Italian family is Sunday dinner. It didn't matter where in the world you were; come high noon on Sunday, it was

---

1 If you don't know what all of these are, you need to start eating better. If you don't know what any of these are, you need to stop reading.

time for obscene gorging. Even when you were on vacation, you never took a vacation from this tradition. And Italian families only take a vacation to places that have a kitchen where they can cook all the meals for themselves. Italian restaurants were never as good as Mamma made it at home, so Italians never went out to eat willingly. If the question is why not go out for another ethnic food? The answer would be why would you ever eat anything besides Italian food? Speaking of vacations, Jersey Italian families take the same friggin' vacation to the same friggin' shore house during the same friggin' week every single year. Every summer was like *Groundhog Day*.

Sunday dinner was a hectic time in the Lembo house. None of my friends understood anything my parents said, even when they were speaking in English, but my friends always made sure to stop in for "a little bit-a of dis" and "a little bit-a of dat." And, just when you couldn't push anymore "dis" or "dat" down to your stomach, you got a little bit more, until your heart stopped. Whenever you faced this overeating trauma, etiquette demanded that you made your way over to the living room sofa[2] and passed out there. There was nothing to worry about; you were experiencing a very common medical condition called an Italian food coma, which went away after a long nap. And just in time for dessert.

To not eat was a serious insult to my mother, our ancestors, and our patron saints. Without proper dispensation from an Italian priest, passing on a meal could be an affront to the Lord himself. Most of my friends who walked in my house soon learned there are Eleven Commandments in Italy: *Thou shall keep on eating*.

Accordingly, if you wanted to stay on good terms with the Almighty (and my mother), you could only enter the Lembo house hungry and only exit after you were visibly fatter. If not, you were not only not welcomed back, you were not going to heaven. Thanksgiving? That's every week in Italian households with bushels of pasta being served instead of turkey. What about the real Thanksgiving Day? That is the day Italians serve turkey. And bushels of pasta.

Mamma Lembo had one personal commandment of her own: *Thou shall not be late*. The one time I was late for Sunday dinner was the only time. She broke her largest wooden spoon over my head. My brother spent an hour separating my hairs to pluck splinters from my scalp like a chimpanzee removes ticks from one of their young. I'm living proof that to an Italian mother, it is much less sinful to steal a trillion dollars than to arrive late for Sunday dinner.

2 Yes, it was covered in plastic. We called it a *couch condom*.

The worst part about being raised in an Italian family is attending wakes and funerals. These catastrophic events are the most extraordinary displays of misery you'll witness anywhere on the planet. Unlike other funerals, where sad attendees stand around and whisper with one another about fond memories of the recently deceased, Italians at funerals don't say anything to each other. It's forbidden by the Italian bible. Everyone must stand or sit silently at an Italian funeral, staring blankly forward like zombies. Under Italian regulations, only your newly widowed aunts are allowed to wail, "TAKE-A ME!" and "WHY-A?"

Please don't ask them if they are okay. They will never be okay. Why? All uncles who lived for over 95 years die tragically and suddenly too young according to Italian tradition. Apparently 75 years of marriage is "not fair" enough. My non-Italian friends were always fascinated and understandably a bit traumatized by the theatrics. They would call me the next day and ask questions like, "Was that your Aunt Connie who got into the casket and shook the corpse like he was only sleeping?"

Then you had the post-burial dress code that consisted of black everything. Black is always the new black after an Italian husband kicks the can. My widowed aunts wore black shoes, socks, underwear, girdles, bras, hats, nail polish, sunglasses, scarves, and dresses for a dozen years after their husbands passed. Ninjas dressed more colorfully than my aunts in mourning.

My parents were old school. They believed in two types of discipline: the shoe and the belt. It all depended upon which was closer in proximity at the time I fucked up. Nowadays, you're not permitted to use corporal punishment on kids. Back then—or at least back then in the Lembo house—no law could possibly save you. No wonder I developed such disdain for the law later on in life. Where was the law when I was getting the strap? My parents didn't punish me. They beat me. I never went to my room for a timeout to *think about what I did*. I went there to cry from the ass pounding I just took. Young Christians were safer in the Colosseum than inside the Lembo Juvenile House of Pain. To this day, I swear that my mother choreographed the beating scenes from the movie *The Passion of the Christ* the time that I stole her car.

At least Mamma Lembo gave fair warning. Prior to any beat downs, she would always shout a predetermined fate like Caesar himself:

"If I-a catcha you-a smoking again, I'm-a gonna tie you to da tree, and light-a you tongue-a on-a fire!"

Or, "If you-a not-a home-a by 10 o'clock, I am-a gonna stick dis-a broom-a up-a you ass-a until-a you-a look-a like-a pop-a-sicle!"

My old man has worked as a carpenter since he was six months old so he had a far more potent arsenal of weapons to throw at me. He was, by far, the quicker, quieter draw. No advance directives were issued to put you on notice. Pops had the strength and accuracy of the mighty Thor with his hammer, so I always maintained a fifty-yard minimum radius from him whenever I was up to no good.

Poppa Lembo was a no-nonsense, hard-working immigrant who was not afraid to cry or beat you until you did. *Bread on the table* was the motto of his life. Orazio Lembo, Sr. came from nothing, arrived in America with nothing, married early, had two kids early, and earned every dollar with his hands while speaking a broken language[3] in a foreign land. All he ever wanted was a quiet life to provide for his family.

Once his last son and namesake, Orazio Jr., was born into the world, the dream ended.

My father had no expensive tastes and no bad habits, unless you count the occasional cruel and unusual punishment he dished out on my backside. To him, a stripper is something you used to remove paint. Hookers are attached to the end of fishing lines. Coke comes in two-liter bottles. I watched him struggle for everything he earned and like to think I inherited his intense work ethic. But I had a ton of bad habits, expensive tastes, manicured hands, and aspired to have a hell of a lot more bread on my table.

And my hands-on approach to earning was based on sleight of hand.

---

3 While quite handy, he still has not fixed his broken language to this day.

TWO

I STARTED DOWN MY PATH TO CRIMINAL INFAMY AS...*wait for it*...a newspaper delivery boy! It was my first and last completely legitimate job. It was also the beginning of my lifelong obsession with collecting money. Every Monday, I would leave all my subscribers an envelope addressed to them that included the amount they owed, with a "plus tip" remark next to a hand-drawn smiley face. I instructed them to leave the same envelope containing their payment by Friday, and no later than Friday, either in their mailbox or under their doormat. This gave them plenty of time to remember the small amount they owed me, so there would be no complaints or questions. I know this seems like excessive measures for such small potatoes, but those payments were worth a million bucks to me and I was fanatical about not getting beat for a single penny.

If someone was two weeks' delinquent, or *forgetful* as they called it, I immediately changed their account to *collection* status. No exceptions, not even for relatives, who would never pay unless you held a rapier to their throat. At that point, clients in collection status would get a new pet—me sitting on their front steps every single day like a loyal dog as they arrived home from work. This way, they were forced to see me and therefore deal with me, prior to entering their home. If they were late from work, I stayed late at their home. Time never mattered to me when it came to money. I stood for hours to collect a few bucks. It wasn't the few bucks that I was investing my time in. It was the message. And the message eventually got through.

Over time, I became a neighborhood fixture on certain people's stoops. If I was sick and was owed ten bucks, I was sneezing on someone's steps. If I had a baseball game, I was late because I was waiting on someone's steps. I froze on people's steps. I sweated on people's steps. If I had to go to the bathroom, I held it in on someone's steps. If I had homework—well, I never did that even when I wasn't owed money. Sooner or later, all the other neighbors knew why young Ozzy was sitting on someone's steps when they passed by. This created visible consistency and, most importantly, it established my street credibility. Sure, it was more like Sesame Street credibility looking back, but I was purposefully a pain in the ass when someone owed me money and that was the message I strove to convey: *if you want to read the headlines, you've got to pay the messenger!* Not quite Don Corleone, but close enough for a 13-year-old.

One day, while I was perched on a stoop waiting for a two-dollar delinquent to come home, I noticed Nina walking home from school across the street.[4] She was crying. Behind her were three boys from my neighborhood laughing and teasing her. One boy was much bigger than the other two. Nina was a sweet and innocent little girl. More importantly, she also happened to come from a *connected* family. Everyone in the neighborhood knew this, except the three morons who were making fun of her that day.

Regardless of whom she was related to, seeing Nina cry enraged me. I hated bullies. Instinctively, I rolled up a thick set of newspapers as tightly as I could. Tightness was the key. I learned that the hard way being on the receiving end of many of Mamma Lembo's homerun swings. Once my bat was ready, I walked calmly across the street.[5]

Walking with my unassuming head down, I was not an imposing figure, which was exactly the cover I needed. As I was hoping (maybe praying), the

4 Let me be upfront with you—this is not leading to sex. However, I promise all the other girls I introduce from this point on will. Except one.
5 I learned calmness before an attack the hard way: from Poppa Lembo's surprise attacks.

bullies ignored me as I approached them. When I got close enough, I wound back and smacked the largest of the three with my newspaper bat as hard as I could squarely on the nose. It exploded in blood and he went down hard from the sudden impact and hit his head on the sidewalk, which further dazed him. I proceeded to pound him repeatedly, cursing the whole time like I was Joe Pesci. Again and again, I whacked his head and face with as much force as I could until there was basically nothing left of my paper bat. My onslaught literally tattooed the ink from the newspaper all across his face. The bully was now a bloody billboard of the day's headlines.

When he finally managed to get to his feet, he ran away from me sobbing. As for his friends? Thankfully, they did exactly what I was hoping for—darted off as soon as they witnessed my surprise assault on their leader.

I turned around and noticed Nina was now on her grandfather's front porch. She saw what I did to her tormentors and smiled at me with tears still welled up in her eyes. Her grandfather stepped outside and I could see her telling him what I just did for her. He put on his glasses and looked me over. My bloody, frayed weapon was still in my hand. I didn't say anything to him. I turned away, dropped my bat into a garbage can, and began to walk back to my collection station as calmly as before. With my back turned, I heard him ask Nina, "Who's that kid anyway?"

Nina replied, "You know Grandpa, the paperboy across the street!"

His reply was one that would basically stick with me for the rest of my life. "You mean the collection kid?" And so I was labeled.

A few days later, Uncle Louie, the Italian monarch of my newspaper territory and beyond, stopped his long-nosed Cadillac in the middle of a street and whistled me over while I was delivering my route on my bike. I approached him trying to appear way more secure than I actually felt.

Through a waft of cigar smoke Uncle Louie asked me, "Hey, collection kid, you want a better job?" It had the structure of a question but his tone made it sound more like a command.

"What kind of job?" I asked.

"Same thing you're used to, kid. Collections."

"Umm, who will I be working for?" *Dumb question, I know.*

"Me! Who else?"

Fuck yeah! I screamed out in my head. Talk about the promotion of a lifetime. And I was still just a teenager.

"Sure," I said, trying to conceal my orgasm.

In my neighborhood—and scattered throughout all of New Jersey and Staten Island—were two types of wiseguys. You had your wannabe wiseguys. These posers were meathead, juicehead guidos who walked around with their arms out from their body acting like they're tough because they knew someone who was connected. Why did these tanned imbeciles believe they were tough guys? Because their last name and gym mirrors told them so. Watch MTV's *Jersey Shore* and you'll get the picture. Then there were the real wiseguys. They're an endangered species today, but back then, this was a select group of older men who never acted tough and rarely talked tough. You never heard anyone from the neighborhood discuss them or how tough they were, even in a whisper. But somehow we all knew who the toughest son of a bitch was. And now the toughest one of all was my new boss.

"Is Uncle Louie here?" I meekly asked the man behind the pizza counter a week later. My mind was racing with anticipation, fear, and excitement faster than I was able to pedal my way to my new job. This was not quite like any other first day on the job.

"You must be the collection kid," the pizza man told me. "Follow me."

As soon as the door opened to the back room, I walked into my first *front*. You never forget your first front. Through the door behind me was a small pizzeria with a few customers. In front of me, in this hidden room, sat a dozen or so husky Italian men puffing cigars, sipping espresso, counting money, playing cards, and watching horse races.

Over time, I would learn that all of them had nicknames given by their peers that mostly highlighted their worst trait. There were the obvious ones, like Cheap Tommy, Bald Angelo, and Paulie the Nose. Others referred to the business they were in, like Charlie Meats or Johnnie Lumber. Some nicknames were not so apparent at first, like Vinnie Radio, which made sense only after I heard for myself that Vinnie never shut the fuck up. Then you had my favorite, the reverse nicknames, like calling the biggest man in the group Tiny Pete.

In the rear of the room there was a large glass window revealing an enclosed office where Uncle Louie sat behind a desk. He wore a colorful collared shirt like the rest of his crew. Thick reading glasses covered most of his face. When I walked inside his office, he was looking over paperwork with a bunch of numbers on it like a typical accountant or mafia capo.

"You found it," he said to me without looking up.

"Sure did," I replied, staring down at the same paper he was looking at.

Still not looking up, he instructed, "This is where you report to work."

"Okay."

Then his mood changed as he glared right into my eyes, "I'm only going to say this once kid, so pay very close attention to me—"

My eyes widened and my toes curled under in my shoes. Even my bowels shifted into position so they were ready to soil my pants. I never paid more attention in my entire fuckin' life, which I was afraid may be ending.

Uncle Louie pointed his pen down at his desk and proclaimed, "What happens here, kid, stays here!"[6]

On one hand, it was a perfectly clear statement to me. On the other hand, it was not because I was not exactly sure yet what "happens here." But I knew I would learn soon enough. That made me excited and nervous.

For my first week, Fat Tony trained me. You already can picture what he looked like, but let me be more specific: Fat Tony was so fat that the really fat guys nicknamed him Fat Tony. He was also filled with life lessons including, "for fuck's sake, don't ever get married"[7] and other advice as he drove me around the neighborhood, showed me my route, and walked me through all the procedures. As it turned out, I was inheriting some of his route. I didn't say it out loud, but I figured it was so he would have more time to eat. At close to 500 pounds, Fat Tony took a week to get in and out of his Cadillac. He was way too slow moving for my jackrabbit speed, so after a week I told him I was ready. And, just like that, I was on my own.

Each day after school, I was given a list of customers along with their names, addresses, amounts owed, and sometimes a remark such as "no less." I peddled my bicycle (that's right—I said bicycle, not motorcycle, not even moped) house-to-house picking up money and placing it into envelopes. I

---

6 Uncle Louie should have copyrighted that slogan because years later, Las Vegas tourism stole it from him without permission and made a killing from it. Of course, their meaning was not quite the same as his.

7 I'm still following this bit of advice to this very day.

recorded each customer's name, date, time, and payment amount. None of this was unlike my paper route except that I was hauling so much cash that I had to develop my first *front* of many more to follow in my life. This front was my old canvas newspaper sack. I asked my seamstress mother—Italian moms cook, sew, and freeze food better than anyone—to sew a hidden zipper compartment inside the bag so that it would be separate from where the newspapers were located. Of course, she thought I was still delivering the neighborhood news, which was still sort of accurate, except I was delivering only bad news now. The front of the bag carried the newspapers. The hidden compartment was stuffed with cash.

Sometimes I was given very specific instructions like "stay." That meant stay in the house of the customer, even if it was burning, until I collected. Period. For these jobs, I didn't sit outside on front steps and wait. I was instructed to sit inside these living rooms, watch TV, make myself comfortable, and even take a nap if I wanted. But I had to remain in the house and was not permitted to leave until the full required payment was in my hands.

It was awkward for the customers, but to me it was an empowering experience, not to mention comical, especially when customers lied about who I was to other family members and guests. I was happy to play along with their lies. In fact, those days were my training days for the thousands of impersonations that were to come later on. I was *a cousin staying over.* I was *a boy from down the block locked out of his house.* One teacher said I was there *to be tutored.* One time, I was *a homeless kid.* Mostly, I was a friend of one of the children who were typically nowhere near my age or some kid I never met.

I loved every one of these charades. Once upon a time, I was the little dog freezing outside on your porch looking for the few bucks you owed me. Now, I was a Great fucking Dane lying down on your couch in the middle of your living room not moving until you fed me thousands of your dollars.

All the customers on my new route were gamblers. Within the first few days, I noticed the vicious cycle: my clients were always chasing losses from prior weeks or borrowing from one loan shark to pay another loan shark. Incidentally, all were under Uncle Louie's criminal umbrella. Gamblers routinely fell behind on payments and consequently fell into the danger zone. What was so worth the grave risk? They would tell me it's the *thrill.* What fucking *thrill*? You weren't even playing in the fucking game! You were betting your own mortgage money on millionaires playing a kids game they didn't even give a shit about! Don't even get me started on betting ponies or slot machines. Fucking pathetic.

I watched it firsthand and realized early on that gambling is the worst vice to have. Believe me, I am an expert on vices so pay attention. The primary reason gambling is the worst of all bad habits is because no amount of money affords a gambling addiction. At least with cocaine, I knew how much my habit cost me each day and could budget accordingly. Hookers come with set prices, too. In fact, drugs and hookers are helpful tools for improving your budgeting skills, as they require payment upfront for blow and blowjobs, respectively. Even drinking is better for financial planning purposes. You can only drink so much whiskey in a day until you run out of money, pass out, die, or can't stop telling everyone you never really liked how much you love them. But gambling—that is a bottomless money pit. At least drinking, coke, and hookers deliver *highs* every time.[8]

No amount of income in the world can keep up with the habit of a degenerate gambler because whatever you make, you stake. The very nature of gambling forces you to double down until you end up too far down, and in some cases, six feet down. Gambling also destroys everything around it. Big time gamblers borrow and steal from everyone around them. They fuck over all their friends. They never stay married. They can't hold down a job. Before you judge the other vices just as harshly, know this—I know dozens of other degenerate addicts who have great wives, lives, and jobs. You may be one of them or know one of them. *None of them* are degenerate gamblers and you can bet your ass on that!

The stress is also worse for gamblers. Every day you are chasing, running, or hiding. If you are ahead for the week, you're chasing losses from the week before. If you are behind for the week, you're chasing to get even. You become a slave to your bookie's gambling schedule. Every Thursday, there are two options: you either get paid or you have to pay up. Well, there's also the third option: you disappear. Your whole world revolves around Thursday's looming deadline, not to mention having to sit up late each night to watch west coast games you bet on. Gamblers are always stressed watching a sporting event that no one else gives a shit about, even the players. All that aggravation, all that money, and for what? Don't tell me there is nothing like the feeling of winning money. Men who believe that never snorted an eight ball and had a threesome with Brazilian-waxed Slovakian strippers with great tit jobs. So stay away from

8 Unless you spot an Adam's apple, which, by then, is usually too late.

your Uncle Louie and listen to your Uncle Ozzy: Choose your vices wisely, boys and girls. Stick to getting laid or high (or both!) and you'll always be a winner.

Degenerates and wiseguys schooled me in the harsh ways of the streets—how to make money, hide it, collect it, launder it, lend it, and spend it. Physically, I may have been a scrawny, awkward adolescent, but when I knocked on your door, I was 6'5" and 300 pounds of twisted fuckin' hot steel. No one wanted me knocking because you knew who I was knocking for. During those days, I came to understand how an undercurrent of power controlled and profited off the weaknesses and vulnerabilities of people. This was real power—the kind that ruthless men of the underworld imposed on their fellow neighbors. I learned the importance of being useful and trustworthy. I saw the value of bestowing favors to establish key connections. I sharpened and honed my collecting skills to better serve my boss. I became an expert in dishonest customer relations. All of these lessons and skills served me for the rest of my scheming life.[9]

Those were the days I first felt that rush from threatening asshole delinquents who were avoiding me and I had learned to do it without raising my hands or voice. I mastered intimidating big hulking contractors whose checks bounced. I could diplomatically persuade stubborn men, much older than me, to give me what I needed. I learned how to properly address and then manipulate these debtors' bosses, wives, and children. I perfected the role of being both someone's best friend and their worst enemy. I never got upset or excited nor did I ever project fear, even when I was shitting-my-pants scared. My personality and poise measured far beyond my years—coolly tenacious and most of all, meticulously organized when it came to records. I think I was the most organized employee in the history of organized crime. In case you don't know, the mob doesn't recognize Employee of the Month with a plaque and dinner at Applebee's. They show their appreciation by giving you more and more responsibilities. And cash. And that's exactly what Uncle Louie did with me. And that's exactly what I wanted.

---

9 That is, until I got busted, of course.

THREE

MEANWHILE AT MY HIGH SCHOOL, MY SOCIAL CAREER STARTED TO BOOM. The boys took respectful notice of me, even the upper classmen who typically ignore lower class boys while they mercilessly poach their grade's best looking babes for their own pleasures. What was more exciting was the fact that the best-looking girls in all the grades began taking their clothes off for me. So, please don't blame me for turning into a certifiable sex addict; blame my female high school classmates. They started it!

I was not the best looking guy in school in anyone's opinion—except my own—but the unspoken secret that I was connected to Uncle Louie was certainly no secret in the halls of my high school. I was not a Jedi yet, or, as the mob terms it, *made*; however everyone, including me, assumed I would be soon down the road. For now, I was the next best thing to it: I was connected. And being connected made my peers want to be connected to me. Life taught me very early what it eventually teaches everyone—it's all about whom you know, never about what you know. Perhaps nowhere is this lesson better proven than in the mob and in high school.

By my sophomore year, I started running my own *book* and soon controlled all the gambling throughout the school. Starting with simple *4-picks-for-4-bucks* football bets, I proudly recruited lifetime degenerate gamblers for Uncle Louie's rackets. Crimes are like drugs; there's always a gateway. So gambling led to dealing a little pot and then some coke and then selling a weapon or two here and there. During that time, I rehearsed and perfected the character that I would play for the rest of my life. I became "Ozzy", a smooth talking, head banging, go-to guy for all your favorite 80s vices: weed, acid, coke, 'shrooms, guns, and the Minnesota Vikings plus 7. Even some of my teachers became customers. You know, it turns out studying is not the easiest way to passing.

And of course, I also began to experiment more and more with the *high* part of high school.

The minute I was seventeen years old, I bought a shiny new Chrysler Conquest for cash. I had thousands more stashed in the drop ceiling of my basement bedroom, which financed all kinds of raging hormonal *high* jinks. During those days, I was regularly sneaking out of my parents' house during late hours of the night to get high or sneaking in girls to get laid. You see why I love my music loud? I figured my parents preferred hearing Ronnie James Dio scream through the ceiling rather than our neighbor's teenage daughter.

Hysteria. Bad. A Momentary Lapse of Reason. Appetite for Destruction. These were not just album titles released in the 80s—they were my way of life. The Ozzy Lembo Crazy Train of sex, drugs, cash, and heavy metal had officially left the station and was never turning back. *All aboard*!

As soon as I could drive a car, I was promoted to the company's *office*. My bicycle was retired permanently. It belongs in the Smithsonian for Crime, if you ask me. Anyway, the office I was promoted to is better described as a bookie boiler room and it was in a Bronx apartment that processed much of the illegal sports wagering in northern New Jersey.[10]

What about the police? Well—they were actually good at busting us.

10 That office (and all other bookie boiler rooms) had what we call *legs,* and those legs are used to change locations every month or so. The phone numbers change with the office location. There is always a contingency office ready somewhere in case of a raid or bust. While my friends were working in commercial buildings that had fire safety training drills, I worked covertly in apartments and was drilled to destroy evidence, get away, and be up and running at another location within an hour.

By that, I mean good at letting us know they were coming so we could not be there. On occasion, we would need to leave behind a sacrificial lamb or two to be arrested together with a few grand to be confiscated. Our selected perpetrators would eventually get let off easy with a fine or short probation. Of course, the bust never went further than one or two of our willing patsies. Why would someone volunteer to get arrested? For one, they were handsomely compensated. Secondly, they had no choice. But this was good public relations all around. For the mob and the cops.

During my Bronx days, I would visit my hometown friend Mikey who was studying pre-law at Fordham University. Mikey's father was a well-connected, highly respected *businessman* from Brooklyn, who later was busted as a tycoon in New York City's heating oil rackets. Those were the days Mayor Rudy Giuliani was locking up every businessman whose last name ended in a vowel (like his), in industries ranging from garbage to construction to oil to the fish market. Interestingly, I do not recollect our "tough on crime" mayor targeting anyone in the most corrupt industry in all of New York: politics. *Look over there, voters! There's certainly nothing to see over here.*

Mikey's old man swam in the same waters with the same fish I worked for so he knew exactly what I was doing and whom I was doing it for. Whenever I saw him, he made it a point to tell me that he was not happy about my choices. I couldn't be happier about my choices so I did my best to avoid seeing him. Either way, I knew he was keeping tabs on me but I never fully realized how much he would end up changing the trajectory of my life until much later.

One night, Mikey met me for dinner at our favorite restaurant, Dominick's, located in the Bronx's Little Italy. He dropped a book bag next to me and sat down. I asked him, "What's this?"

"It's your school bag. Inside is your nighttime class schedule for this semester, plus a Fordham sweater, t-shirt, and hat."

"What the fuck do I need this shit for?"

"Because you need a legitimate fucking reason for going over the George Washington Bridge every night at the same time and coming back in a few hours other than your daily blowjobs, dime bags, and running numbers out of Arthur Avenue."

Mikey was being serious so he deserved a sincere response from me. "I need to tell you something. I'm out of the closet now and would love to come back to your dorm and blow you in front of all your college roommates."

"Keep the fucking bag in the front seat and wear something from it each time you travel here. Memorize the schedule and show it to the police if you get pulled over. Next semester, I will get you a new one."

I went on in my life to deal with thousands of lawyers. But from that moment on, Mikey was the only lawyer I ever trusted, even when I hated him. Mikey was right about the risk. Our biggest problem in the bookie business wasn't volume. Degenerates regenerate rapidly from generation to generation. If you just look around, you'll find them everywhere, including your hometown and maybe even inside your home. Discreet transportation was our problem, namely the handling and transporting of large amounts of betting slips or *numbers,* as we called them. This shit-ton of nightly paperwork was the smoking gun of our crime and too voluminous to easily conceal. To further complicate matters, promoting gambling in the (Criminal) Empire State of New York was a misdemeanor, punishable by a slap on the wrist of community service and a fine. *Okay. So that's not too bad.* However, on the other side of the bridge, in the (Thorny and Horny) Garden State of New Jersey, the same exact offense was a felony that carried serious prison time. *Ouch!*

Who would have guessed that yours truly was an excellent underground office manager? At first, I took bets over the phones like everyone else but I quickly rose up in the ranks. With my quick wit and focus on details, I shined brightly on the Dark Side. Okay, admittedly the brightest bulbs on the criminal Christmas tree didn't exactly surround me during those early years.[11] Before I knew it, I was basically in charge of all operations and thus labeled myself the *CACO,* Chief Administrative Criminal Officer. My job was to oversee and implement the most efficient protocols and processes to execute hundreds of crimes per night without a hitch. *King of the Morons* was the unofficial title I gave myself.

My superior intelligence and sense of humor among these morons could not mask the sobering fact that if I fucked up—more than if anyone else fucked up—it would be catastrophic to my racketeering bosses. Accordingly, despite what Mikey was concerned with, I wasn't the least bit afraid of the police catching me crossing the George Washington Bridge. My only fear was they would find me floating under it one morning.

So here's how this racket works: when a customer phoned in, he was

11 Did I mention yet that *wiseguys* is the most misleading term ever coined?

required to begin the exchange by stating his codename. For example, "This is Iceman for Maverick." "Maverick" was the runner name that the caller was connected to. I was one of the runners and "Iceman" was the specific code name given for that specific customer. As long as Iceman's account was in good standing, i.e., paid to date, he was allowed to place a wager on any sports event, such as who would win, what the spread was, what round someone would get knocked out in, or who would win the fucking coin flip in a bowl game.

As his runner, I was 100% responsible for Iceman's account. Even if he lost, I won. *Sounds good, eh?* Well, not when he lost and didn't pay. Then I was responsible to cover his debt 100%, including any *vig*, meaning the bookie's cut, and points added on for any delinquency. It was also my responsibility to collect the money from him. That is why runners like me needed to be *very* selective about choosing their Icemen because if they ever hit an iceberg, you were guaranteed to sink with them.

Typically, your Iceman had his own little business network of which he was the responsible party for and subsequently took a cut from. You can see how multi-level marketing works in both legal and illegal businesses. The fewer people a runner had to deal with, the better. To clarify, as Maverick, I would prefer a $10,000 single bet by one "Goose" to a ten $1,000 bets by a gaggle of geese.

Generally, all of my customers were people from my neighborhood and high school. I never took on a player that I didn't know personally or that someone I trusted did. One degree of separation was as far as I would go in my bettor network. Other greedier, more reckless runners would cross all the degrees to Kevin Bacon to make a quick buck. For my illicit web, I stuck to close friends and close friends of friends. Friendships were a basis for taking someone into my network. However that same friendship never stopped me from cutting them out whenever they were short by even one nickel. I made it clear upfront that my business was as serious as a heart attack and potentially more lethal than that to any one of my friends.

Now back to the phones. Once a customer was cleared to bet, he was asked, "How can I help you?" The customer would reply something like, "How are the Steelers?" and the operator would check the *line* (also known as *odds*) on the game that was posted in front of him on a huge whiteboard. The line was set by Las Vegas, not us, and could be found in any newspaper under "Vegas line" in the sports section. (This gives a bit of insight into how widespread underground gambling actually is in the United *Stakes* of America.) The operator would indicate the point spread and the favorite in a specific way. Suppose the Steelers were playing the Cowboys, and the Steelers were favored by six points. Instead of all that verbiage, we would simply utter, "Pittsburgh is minus six." It always went by whomever the favorite was minus the point spread, or odds. Once the customer made his wager, the operator would fill out a slip including the customer's codename, his runner's info, and the wager amount, which we referred to as *times*.

Times is code for the amount to be wagered times five. If you took the Pittsburgh Steelers minus six points over the Dallas Cowboys for $500, you would say "Give me Pittsburgh minus the six, 100 times"—and then hope like hell that the Steelers won by more than six points. Protocol demanded that you repeat your code once again, "Iceman for Maverick", as the conversation was recorded while the betting slip was filled out, containing the wager information, date, and time. The date and time on the slip corresponded to the tape that the wager was recorded on, in case there was a discrepancy on the team bet or the amount played.

The whole process went much faster than it just took me to explain it. And I broke it down for you that way to illustrate a larger point—if the transactions seem confusing, think about how difficult it was to keep track of hundreds of those transactions every single night, 365 nights a year. That is why *booking* is a bookkeeping nightmare. We opened, closed, and reconciled our books every day. If, God forbid for him, a player missed a payment, you needed to add on interest payments, which were ten points, not per annum, not monthly, but every single week *ad infinitum*.[12] When you were directed to remove someone's debt, you were unsure whether to be happy for him that he paid or unhappy for his family that he didn't.

All that paperwork, plus corresponding tapes, would be loaded into large black garbage bags and transported back to Uncle Louie's joint in New Jersey at the end of the evening's take. This was typically my job and was a dangerous nightly expedition, every single night of the year. Gambling gets no holidays because gamblers take no holidays. In fact, holidays were the busiest gambling days of the year. *Merry fucking Christmas!*

You now see why the handling and delivery of the slips was the highest

12 meaning *always up your ass* in Latin

priority and greatest risk of our entire racket. It contained hard information critical to the underworld as it served as the proof for the men above me who were splitting the profits. Wiseguys honor and respect one another, but they never trust each other. Trust me on this.

After going through a couple of pinches and raids, I thought of an idea, one that would greatly enhance my stature in the underworld.

I visited Uncle Louie and told him that I had a plan to eliminate the risky paper trail. It was easier for me to just show him rather than explain it to him. To accomplish showing him, I needed a furnished apartment in the same building where the office was located and a list of supplies that I dropped in front of him on a sheet of paper. As he looked at the paper, he asked, "Tell me, kid, where the fuck are you going with this?"

I looked him straight back in the eyes. "I'll show you. Just trust me."

He did. Less than a week later, he tossed me a pair of keys and said, "507." I caught the keys and smiled.

As I strode out like John Travolta on 86th Street, he said, "Hey kid, make me proud." Now don't confuse that statement with a warm sentiment of encouragement from my mentor. Uncle Louie was warning me.

I turned back around at the doorway. "Don't I always?"

Apartment 507 was on a floor above the bookie boiler room. When I opened the door to the apartment, I was pleased to see all the items on my list right there in the middle of the living room—a computer, a printer, two fax machines, a huge box of cassettes including everything from Aerosmith to ZZ Top, a leather cassette carrying case, pair of aluminum garbage cans, lighter fluid, paper, scissors, and scotch tape. I asked another runner, Jimmy Two Dimes,[13] to come up to 507 with me to help set up because he was the smartest of the morons I worked with.

"Take all of these cassettes out of their cases," I instructed Jimmy. "Put a piece of tape over both of the holes on the top of the cassette then put the cassette back into its corresponding case."

Jimmy nodded, so I continued, "When you're done, take the garbage cans and the lighter fluid up to the roof and then bring these cassettes down to the office and place one in each recorder on side A. Leave the case right next to the

---

13 His nickname referred to the fact that much of what Jimmy said could be answered with "get two dimes and call someone who gives a shit."

recorder. Then come back up here; okay?"

"You got it, Oz," Jimmy replied, nodding and then added, "You know, Oz, I like the way that guy in ZZ Top grows his beard and..."

Two fucking dimes, Jimmy!

I set up the fax machines and the computer software. Back then there was no Microsoft, which meant no Windows. Everything was DOS, and for the spreadsheet, it was Lotus 1-2-3. You see students—you *can* learn something in school that benefits you later in life. For me, it was committing major felonies using Lotus 1-2-3. My Intro to Computers teacher would have been so proud.

Jimmy returned to me and announced, "Mission accomplished." I handed him one of the fax machines with the settings already in place and told him to head to the Uncle Louie's restaurant with it. Before he left, I explained to him how to count pages. This was an important step and not an easy one, even for a high-performing moron like Jimmy, because early fax machines had only curl-up paper in them.

By that time, the last game for the night already started, so there were no more bets coming in. I headed down to the office and took the bag containing all the night's slips. I then ejected each cassette by each phone station, put it back in the original case, and headed back up to Room 507.

Now it was time for data entry. Slowly and methodically, I entered each and every wager into the spreadsheet on the computer. It included the customer name, runner name, amount of the wager, wager itself, and the exact time and date. I also included who wrote the slip and what cassette the wager corresponded with. Once all data was entered (not a quick task to accomplish), I then reconciled the slips with the total amount of wagers on the spreadsheet (another exhaustive task). Thankfully, it *washed*, which is wiseguy code for matched.

I called Jimmy. He was waiting patiently at the Uncle Louie's restaurant still without a clue as to what was going on. I imagined the whole Uncle Louie calling him a dumb shit, standing there with the fax machine and not knowing why. Looking back, those were primitive communication days, but that night I felt like Scotty ready to beam Captain Kirk onto the surface of Saturn. I took the 25-page report now on my dot matrix printer paper, cut the pages to fit into the send slot of the fax machine, and pressed send. *Ring! Beeeep!* And away the sheets went!

Several minutes later, Jimmy called. "Hey Oz—it's Jimmy. Twenty-five pages?" he asked me excitedly.

"Yes. We're good," I replied calmly. "Jimmy, did Uncle Louie see the fax?"

"He has it in his hands as we're talking."

Uncle Louie grabbed the phone, "Kid, you're a fucking genius!" I'm certain Jimmy still had no clue about what just transpired in front of his eyes, but Uncle Louie understood what I revolutionized when he looked at what I just sent him seemingly through thin air. *Un-patrolled thin air.*

"Get your ass here," he told me and hung up.[14]

With that, I darted up to the building's roof carrying the garbage bag of slips. I dumped out all the papers in the bags into the can, saturated it with lighter fluid, and dropped in a match. *Now that's a fire!* While the felony exhibits burned away beautifully into the starry sky, I couldn't help myself from snapping my fingers and belting out Dion... *here's my story. It's sad but true...* Why? Because that is what you do over a burning garbage can in the Bronx, even when you're alone and in the commission of a felony.

Once the slips burned completely away, I went back to Jersey with the leather cassette case containing my music (read: *gambling*) library. Forty-five minutes later, I strutted into Uncle Louie's office and placed the leather case on top of his desk. As he stared at it, I opened it up and handed him one of my personal favorites, Aerosmith's *Toys in the Attic.*

"What's this?" he asked.

"Just put on these headphones and listen to side A."

I left him there and walked out singing, "Sweeeeet Emoooootion," knowing Uncle Louie was shaking his head in amazement behind me listening to all the evening's bets. His young apprentice had single-handedly solved the biggest problem the industry faced with crossing the border between New York and New Jersey. I was so proud of myself. I thought about how impressed and proud Uncle Louie must have been at that moment.

And I knew I had just punched my ticket to being the youngest made man in Uncle Louie's crew.

---

14 By the way, wiseguys always politely kiss each other hello in person, but never say goodbye when they hang up. They just hang up. Even on their family. Sometimes they do it when the other person is still speaking. At first, you think you got cut off. You didn't. Well, actually, you did get cut off—intentionally by the higher-ranking party. I was never really sure why about the abrupt hang ups, but it became part of my phone etiquette for life.

FOUR

T EIGHTEEN, I HAD BUCKETS OF CASH AND NEEDED SOMETHING TO SPEND MY illegal proceeds on. I also needed to get the hell out of my house. Not that it was a bad place to stay in terms of food, laundry, and shelter. It was just a bad place to get high, stash cash, and have orgies. It was time to find a more natural habitat for my increasingly immoral habits.

I had a lot of cash, but not enough to purchase a bachelor pad outright until I was lucky enough to get in an automobile accident. The proceeds from my resulting fraudulent settlement, combined with my already ill-gotten gains, provided the financial freedom I needed. Do I need to go into how the accident game goes? Okay, quickly then. A dishonest personal injury attorney—I know that's a redundant way to describe him—orchestrated the entire case. Like I said, I had an accident but I really wasn't hurt. However, according to my attorney and the sham doctor he sent me to, I was hurt really bad—physically and, as it turns out, emotionally, too. Who knew? I guess when you're suffering this kind of trauma, you don't realize the whole depth of the pain and suffering you're going through but fortunately for me, my attorney knew and he made sure the defense attorney for the other side knew, too. My pain and suffering from my fake injuries led to a generous out-of-court settlement. Besides receiving said fat payout, I gained insight as to how attorneys operated. It was my first view of lawyers preying upon American society and exploiting others for their personal gain. And I thought the mob was dirty. Lawyers were the apex predators, professional purveyors of pain and suffering. These guys were fucking outlaws with licenses to rob. I made a mental note.

Now, I didn't always spend money, but when I did I spent only cash. Cash was my king. Every deal was easier and cheaper when it was green. Just try it and you'll see. I was all green before it was cool to be environmentally conscious. Hell, I was green before Kermit the fuckin' Frog.

The condo I ended up buying belonged to an ex-wife of a doctor. It was being sold to settle up on their divorce. Since I now had a garbage bag of cash to spend, I was able to negotiate a deal with her for less than market value. In exchange, she got a nice envelope stuffed with 25 grand under the table after the closing that she kept all to herself. Since it was a cash deal with no mortgage, we were able to close within a week. This saved her in time and taxes (which I never paid) and, best of all, gave her the satisfaction of fucking over her ex financially, which I thought was always the best way to get over a breakup.

Conveniently, I showed up at the walkthrough alone. Coincidentally, she was there alone, too. As soon as I walked through the door, I scanned and analyzed the scene like a Sexual Terminator. She was wearing her hair up. *Check*. She had on low-hanging sweatpants. *Check*. A loose shirt was on without a bra. *Check*. She had me by 15 years, which meant we were a perfect match sexually. *Check*. It was 11am and a bottle of wine was half-finished on the counter. *Checkmate!*

As she started telling me how cute I was and how impressed she was with our deal, I casually looked down at my watch and saw what time it was. Time to grab her by the waist, spin her around, rip down her sweatpants, slide her panties to the side—*leave them on, trust me, it's hotter*—and shove my thick Italian sausage inside her baking hot oven from behind. She bossed me around like the little boy I was. She told me to pull her hair, smack her ass, and pin her arms back, while she proceeded to have multiple orgasms all over my soon-to-be new kitchen. It turns out revenge sex with an eighteen-year-old was an even better way to fuck over an ex. I made another mental note. So did my penis.

✦ ◼ ✦

Honestly, moving out at eighteen created a big problem for me. Not that I couldn't afford it, it was the fact that Italian children are not permitted to move out until they marry or die. The only place they are allowed to move to before marriage is the basement and I was already there. I fretted for weeks because I didn't know how to break the news to my mother.

Mamma Lembo is five foot nothing, 140 pounds, and I am scared shitless of her. I knew our relatives in Salerno, Italy, were going to hear her scream about my proposed unauthorized emancipation. The rest of my family was clearly not on my side because I was disrespectfully breaking the Italian umbilical cord prematurely. There was no one in the family who supported me on this; I was totally on my own with this idea.

My predicament perfectly illustrates another larger issue with Italian families: they are littered with hundreds of cousins, aunts, and uncles (many who are not blood-related) and they know *nothing about anything*, yet boldly proclaim to be experts in everything. For some reason, these buffoons always feel compelled to argue baseless opinions loudly, like they are proven facts. I have even witnessed them completely ignore a real expert at the very same dinner table, like a real physician, while they yell incompetently about the causes of obesity or the dangers of smoking. In Italian families, the louder the statement, the wiser it is. Volume trumps substance. Insistence overrules credentials. Name a topic—law, medicine, finance, politics—and I will show you at least two of my blundering relatives who will argue for hours like Nobel laureates on the fucking topic.

Italians are also, by nature, deeply involved in each other's business through hourly contact and a covert network of family spying. If you didn't want your aunt's opinion, she will give it to you anyway. For all these cultural reasons, plus my steady diet of sluts and drugs, I needed to get the hell out of my parents' house and be on my own.

So you can see why I decided not to tell my mother, at least not tell her exactly. She thought I was temporarily housesitting for a friend. My parents tried everything to get me to come home. They offered food every night, cash bribes (to a cash rich son!), and this finally led to them demanding that I go see a shrink because I must be fucking crazy to not want to be home with the family. If I had told any shrink about my crazy family and childhood, the only question would have been *Why the fuck didn't you leave sooner?*

After one year, two months, and twelve days, the housesitting charade finally came to an end. My parents realized that I was never coming home again to live. Not unless a miracle happened…or the government bankrupted me.

Soon thereafter, Uncle Louie summoned me to his office. This time, for the first time, his tone toward me was noticeably different. He directed me to sit and started telling me about how I had a gift and that I needed to use it to do something lucrative…and legal. He said, "Ozzy, I don't want this life for you— you're too smart for this kind of life."

"Why?" I wailed, sounding like one of my widowed aunts. "What am I going to do? I only know how to work for you! I only WANT to work for you!"

With tears in his eyes but an edge in his voice, he barked, "Become a fuckin' lawyer!"

"A lawyer?" I didn't get it. He hated lawyers. I was well on my way to hating them also.

"That's right. A lawyer," he repeated. "Do you know how much I paid lawyers in my lifetime?"

I did not answer because I could tell he was not in the mood for a debate. The last thing he said to me was, "Now get the fuck out of here and go do something better than this shit with your life."

I walked out truly devastated. I was baffled. Angry. No severance. No two weeks' notice. No going away party. No explanation. I'd never skimmed a penny nor cheated him a dime. Thoughts raced through my mind. *What did I do wrong? Did I make a mistake that I was not aware of? Did someone say something untrue about me? Did I say the wrong thing to someone? How can everything I've worked so hard for and taken so much risk for get stripped away without notice or reason? What the fuck am I supposed to do for money now?*

As I got older, it dawned on me. Uncle Louie may have genuinely wanted what was best for me, especially when, not long thereafter, he got sentenced to 65 years and died in prison a decade later. However, he would never, ever have cut me loose for that reason. I was an *earner* and the mob needs earners more than enforcers. The mob needs earners more than they need the air they breathe. No loyal, high earner was ever cut loose in the history of La Cosa Nostra unless there was a compelling reason. And there was only one possible reason compelling enough for my involuntary release—Mikey's father.

He never told me and I never asked, but he was the only one who wanted me out who was influential enough to get me kicked out. No one ever got thrown out of the mob like I did. Exiting a Mafioso's clench was only via a jail cell, witness protection program, or a coffin. Mikey's old man made sure I left alive and without a criminal record.

In the end, he did me the biggest favor of my life.

Or did he?

FIVE

O VER THE YEARS, COLLEAGUES WOULD ASK ME IF I ACTUALLY INVENTED THE art of pretexting. I would tell them no, but Jimi Hendrix didn't invent the guitar either. What I did do was take the art of pretexting to a whole new scorching stratosphere—just like *Purple Haze*, baby—by inventing the *reverse collection*.

"Good evening. This is Officer Jim Blair with the Essex County Sheriff's Department. May I speak with Mr. Joe Gallo?" Back then, there was no Caller ID, so I just had to open up all my conversations by lying convincingly.

"Ummm, this is he." The tone of my target's voice demonstrates he's already nervous. *Good sign*.

"Mr. Gallo, I'm calling because we have a warrant for your arrest—" I pause briefly, pretending to shuffle papers and to allow the target to commence the obligatory shitting his pants before I tell him the really bad news—that I know where he works. "My guys are scheduled to execute it tomorrow at 2:00 pm at the Sears located at the Paramus Park Mall in Paramus, New Jersey. Will you be there at that time, Mr. Gallo?"

Now my target boy Joe is certainly no Boy Scout, but he's not a hardened criminal either—yet. To an expert pretexter, this is the ideal sweet spot for maximizing the fear factor and exploiting the target. "Wait. What? That can't be. There must be some kind of mistake. What did I do? I don't understand!"

Our friend is getting a bit panicky, which means it is time to take command of the situation with calm and certain authority. We want targets scared but not off the rails. "Well, Mr. Gallo, the first thing you need to do is calm down; understand?"

"Okay, okay. I'm sorry." *Good boy.*

"Now, we have a judgment to execute on from a complaint filed by… ummm….give me a second….where is it…it looks like it was filed by a Mr. Michael Hart." Michael Hart was the best wingman I ever had throughout my entire career. And he was completely make believe.

"Michael Hart? I don't know a Mr. Michael Hart!"

"Well, you wrote him a bad check and he filed a complaint."

This clown doesn't have a clue who in the hell Michael Hart is, but Joe has passed bad checks before so this is not his first rodeo. And, more importantly, now he knows that I know. Undoubtedly, Joe's mind is racing to figure out who this guy Michael Hart is and how the hell he's involved with a warrant against him. The time has come for me to be merciful and dangle my bait.

"Mr. Gallo, I ran a warrant search and you came up otherwise clean, so because of that, I will give you a 24-hour courtesy window from right now. If you can somehow work it out with this Mr. Hart and get him to cancel the warrant, then I won't have to send my men over to arrest you at your job." Always instill fear first, and then offer an easier way out; this is the fundamental theory behind all my scams.

"But I don't understand," Joe injects. "How can I do that if I don't know who he is?"

This is when I tell him to get a pen and give him a bogus warrant number. Then, without guaranteeing him it is still valid, I give Joe *my* telephone number as the phone number listed on my papers for Mr. Michael Hart.

And then, one last statement from me to my new bitch Joe (until, of course, we speak again shortly), "So we are clear Mr. Gallo: if I do not receive a written cancel order from Mr. Hart within the next 24 hours, then I will have no choice but to execute on the warrant and lock you up. There will be no more extensions and no more courtesy calls. Are we clear?"

"Yes, we are clear, Officer, and I thank you for giving me the chance to clear this up."

As soon as we hang up, you could not count to ten before the phone rings.

"JDR, how may I help you?" answers one of my team members. Pretexting is most effective when it's a team scam.

"Yes, hello—may I speak with Mr. Michael Hart, please?" *Look at that, Joey's back.*

"What's this regarding, sir?" she probes, digging deeper into his already fragile psyche.

"My name is Joseph Gallo and I am trying to reach Michael Hart on an extremely urgent matter. There's a warrant for my arrest—"

"Okay, then. Have you been arrested yet, Mr. Gallo?" My team is trained to mind-fuck.

"No! No! I mean, not yet. But the police officer said he is coming tomorrow and—"

"Okay, Mr. Gallo, calm down." Her soothing tone implies she wants to be helpful to our target. "I first need a warrant number. Do you have a warrant number?"

"Yes, I do. It's 07514."

"Thank you. Please hold." She then presses the magical collection agency hold-mute button. This magic button allows us to hear what the caller is saying or doing, while the caller listens to country music assuming he's on hold. Often during these times, a sweating debtor will talk to someone else next to him and we'll be able to pick up additional precious information that we'll use to fuck him with later. A minute or so later, I realize our boy Joe is all by his lonesome so I pick up the phone to close out this bitch like Mariano fucking Rivera.

"Michael Hart. How may I help you?" Remember I was just talking to this clown as someone else so now my tone is decidedly lower and older. Like Hendrix, I'm the master of different tones and tunes. *Hey Joe... where ya going to run to now?*

"Yes, Mr. Hart. I'm Joseph Gallo and I got a call from the Essex County Sheriff's department regarding a warrant for my arrest and—"

I cut him off, showing I've got no time or patience for this charade that I created. "Well, tell me what can I do for you?"

"Can you please tell me what this is about, Mr. Hart?"

"Mr. Gallo, don't play games with me. You know exactly what this about. This is regarding the complaint that you ignored that I filed myself personally against you on behalf of my client, Macy's Department Store." *Holy shit, Batman!* My target now gets exactly what is going on. There's been no mistake. Michael Hart is representing Macy's. He knows he did pass a bad check to Macy's and now he believes the law is bearing down on him for it, which is complete and total prime grade bullshit as is this line, "That complaint is for your passage of a bad check. We not only have the check, Mr. Gallo, but we have the video of the crime, so you can expect a visit by the police to arrest you very soon."

"Yes, Mr. Hart, they just called me and said the warrant is going to be executed tomorrow."

"All right then, you're already aware. The only thing I can advise you at this point is that after they arrest you and arraign you at the county jail, you should be able to post the check, fine, and fees the next morning to the court clerk after you see the judge. If you can't, or refuse, to do that, then you'll probably need to post bail to get released."

"You mean either way I'm going to have to spend the night in jail?"

"Yes, but if all goes well, you should be out the next day. From what I understand, at worst it should be no longer than three days. That's as long as the weekend doesn't come first, of course."

"I can't believe this! That is completely unfair!"

"You wrote the check, Mr. Gallo, not me." *Moral indignation has no effect on the devil.*

Now here comes the question that we have all been waiting for. "Is there any way I can pay it now?"

"Now…?" I repeat. "Please hold and I'll check for you." A bong hit later and I return to put an end to his misery and finish him off. "Do you have all the money available now?"

"Well, how much is it?"

Here's the fun part as the question before me is now how much is avoiding three nights in jail worth to our new friend. I start with his original $227.13 check, then slowly and painfully walk him through hundreds more in random filing fees, court costs, attorney fees, interest, and so on. All of those fees are as real as Michael Hart himself is.

"The total is $2,516.44."

"Yes sir, I can do that now!"

BINGO, bitches! "Once we receive payment, I will be able to authorize that the warrant be dismissed."

After he takes our Western Union information, his money hits our account within the hour. Our client Macy's pays us 35% of the collection. Everyone is happy, especially our deadbeat Joe Gallo, who would have begged me to pay off a hundred times his debt after I was done pretexting him. Why chase them to pay you when you can reverse the scenario and get them to chase you so they could pay?

I did that kind of pretext twenty times per day, five days a week at my new job at JDR Recovery. *Reverse Collection 101* created by yours truly, Professor Orazio Lembo.

✦ ◼ ✦

At the time of my mafia expulsion, I was almost twenty and had a difficult time coming to grips with doing something legit. After a lot of soul-searching and head scratching, I finally decided to do something legitimate as illegitimately as I possibly could. I started working at JDR Recovery, a national collection agency, because I already knew how to talk collections on the streets with the best of them.

Working as a paperboy, I knew all my customers and where they lived. Their debts were small and legitimate. I could not impersonate or lie to collect on them, so I decided that making myself enough of a pain in the ass was the only effective way to get people not to ignore me. They paid me, not out of fear, but simply to stop the annoyance.

Working for Uncle Louie, the numbers were much larger and the debtors were less stable, but the power I represented was much more threatening. And threats, implicit or explicit, are the most effective tool in collections. Still, transactions were all conducted one-on-one. For street collections, no check is ever in the mail. No credit card payment is ever made by phone. There is no pay kiosk. No online payments. Cash is the only currency. *Hand it over or else.*

Or else what? The debtors certainly knew what "or else" meant. If I was ignored or given too much of a hard time for too long, I simply told Fat Tony.

At that point the matter was out of my hands—which is exactly what I reminded my obstinate debtors on occasion. Believe me, I was looking out for these bums when I demanded they pay me. Dealing with little ol' Ozzy was much more comforting and easy. Fat "or else" Tony didn't ring your doorbell. He never asked you how your family was doing. He never wanted to know the score of your son's game or how your daughter's dance recital was. There was no small talk with Fat Tony. Fat Tony ate pounds of pasta, took your stuff, and/or seriously hurt you.[15]

In fact, when you saw Fat Tony, he never said anything. He simply barged in without a warrant and confiscated the most expensive personal effects from your home, business, and garage, including your car—especially your car. And hopefully, you had expensive personal possessions for him to take. Fat Tony committed the slowest, most blatant thefts in the middle of the day without saying anything to you. If he had to, he would come to your son's soccer game, approach you on the sidelines while you were coaching and hold out his hand. You knew to reach into your pocket and hand over the keys to your minivan—which he then proceeded to drive out of the parking lot back to your house to load up all your TVs, computers, and jewelry. Sometimes what he took was not enough. Sometimes your vehicles were too old or your wife's diamond earrings were too small. That was the worst kind of "or else."

Uncle Louie told me one man's disappearance teaches every man a lesson for five years. That was the peril and protocol of the business Uncle Louie was running. If one person ever beat the rules, everyone would. Show me a sympathetic collector and I'll show you a broke loan shark. Loansharking is not a charity service. Not paying an Uncle Louie street debt was, in effect, kidnapping a child from him. And he treated you accordingly.

Turns out my street training translated well into quick success in the legitimate collection world. After my first month at JDR, I was already the number two collector for the entire company. Collecting from legitimate deadbeats over the phone was a far cry from dealing with gambling junkies face to face, but I was a natural, and I enjoyed the new challenge. I spent my days at JDR learning the formal rules of the collection business inside and out. I developed a plethora of contacts that I tapped the rest of my life. Most valuably, JDR gave me the ideal audience and platform to test and perfect my characters and unleash them for profit in the collection industry. Through countless hours

15 Add shit, shave, sweat, and snore and there you have the man's entire biography.

of practice on the phone, I mastered dozens of impersonations. By the end of my tenure, I had fashioned myself as a wizard of illusion and, as a result, collected millions in a way no one had ever done before.

Concurrently, the evolution of Ozzy—the notorious party monster— accelerated at light speed during my time at JDR. In the end, it was the character that ultimately consumed me whole as you shall see. During my teenage years, I was like a method actor who tried to never break character in my role as Ozzy. Ozzy was created and first utilized to advance my social stature, mafia status, and the objectives of my penis. He was my cool black leather jacket, covering up all the insecurities and worry teenage boys typically experience. Intoxicants covered up the rest. Then in my twenties, the persona of Ozzy met cocaine. As more and more money and more potent chemicals were added to this equation, Ozzy became a monster that completely took over my reality. And morality. Once Ozzy started inhaling white lines of powder, there was no turning back to Orazio—whoever he was anyway.

The party monster Ozzy became too powerful to be caged and was having too much fun to consider slowing down, even for a contemplative, hungover minute. He provided me the fodder, bullshit, and balls to make all my dreams come true. He certainly deserves all the credit for my induction into the criminal hall of infamy. He also deserves all the blame for taking me down in such spectacular fashion.

SIX

THE COLLECTION BUSINESS IS VERY BIG BUSINESS IN OUR BIG NATION OF defaulters. We all borrow, but not all of us repay, including me. Maybe you innocently forgot to bring back a library book. Maybe you overlooked paying that medical or utility bill. Maybe you never got that job you expected after college so you had to default on your student loans. Maybe you lost that job and had to let your mortgage go unpaid. And maybe, just maybe, you have a valid reason for not paying back your creditors while you enjoy your new flat screen, cell phone, or beach vacation. Valid reasons or not, statistics show there is a very good chance you, as an American, have dealt with a collection matter in your lifetime. Please do not feel badly about this. Embrace it, proudly. After all, owing and not repaying is the patriotic thing to do. *What? You don't agree?* Take a look at the balance sheet of the great USA.

Many people pay off their delinquent debts when they receive a demand letter from a creditor. Others less motivated wait until a phone call comes from someone like me—well, hopefully for you, it wasn't someone quite like me. Some will wait to pay only after the filing of a lawsuit. Still others, totally unconcerned with their credit score, delay paying even longer until they have to pay it involuntarily, such as pursuant to a court-ordered wage garnishment or bank levy. Then you have the cunning dodgers who are so underwater they seek the protection of a bankruptcy court to lawfully extinguish their debts, which doesn't work as well as you may think against someone as unlawfully relentless as me. At the very bottom of the deadbeat pool, you will find the professional *Fuck You* defaulters who have no intention whatsoever of dissolving their debts and choose instead to go *financially underground*, attempting to hide forever from their judgments, garnishments, levies, and obligations. *Fuck You* pros were always my favorite big game to hunt.

I would be remiss if I didn't note that the cost of borrowing money or earning credit for all Americans is impacted by all of this. The more defaults, the higher the costs lenders assume. This gets passed back to the consumer by way of stricter standards and higher borrowing costs. When defaults remain high and uncollected, fewer people are able to borrow less money. People who default are not only screwing over their creditors, they are screwing over everyone else who needs credit.[16]

Now the most valuable commodity of any collection business is current information pertaining to debtors. Information is the backbone of the industry. The more drastic the collection measure, the more information needed to be successful utilizing said measure. Without information, you won't collect. You may only have a name and amount owed from your client to go by. And in America, the land of opportunity and hiding from your responsibilities, a name and amount owed is akin to a needle in a haystack. Information about employment and current residence is essential. When it comes to slippery deadbeats, obtaining either is always a challenge. That is why there are so many people whose fulltime jobs are to find out information about debtors. The goal is to find your target's home or work info so you can contact them via mail or, better still, on the phone. (Some of the great collectors even pay them a visit in person.) Other useful bits in debt collecting include getting information on cars, marital status, spouse's employment, children, schooling, and even family and friends. You can see why all bill collectors, or *information brokers*, are really

---

16 Of course, I never gave two shits about anyone else or the larger financial impact of any of my actions. I was only out to get me some while the gettin' was good. I only point this out to you in case you're the type of person who gives a shit about other people. Personally, I find that never ends up working out for you. Or other people.

just private investigators with a different title.

However, The Holy Grail for debt collecting is in the debtor's banking information. And being able to get that information by any means necessary is why I'm sitting in prison now. But more on that later…

In the legitimate collection business—though you should already see why effective collections can't be completely legitimate—you were either a collector or a skip tracer.[17] A collector is the hunter who uses the phone to terrorize the debtor until he or she gives in and pays up. A skip tracer is the gatherer who retrieves material information on the target debtor, such as phone numbers, jobs, assets, and so on through a multitude of means like credit reports, applications, neighbors, etc. I was both because I love to hunt and I love to gather. The bottom line is the collection industry is a bifurcated business. You first skip trace to locate your target. Then, if successfully located, you turned over your information findings to the collector, who would attempt to collect the debt by either finesse or force. From a collection standpoint, JDR was a finesse firm; Uncle Louie was a force firm.

JDR was where I was first introduced to pretexting, which was like introducing Michelangelo to paint. I was born with an innate talent for telling fairy tales and improvisation, but it was at JDR where I became the undisputed wizard of *pretexting*, which is disguising or lying to someone in order to curry favor or a desired result. Pretexting also has a very similar definition to a more commonly used word that I'm sure you've heard: *bullshit*.

My weapon of mass disruption at JDR was the phone. In order to finesse money out of people's pockets, you need to be versatile, flexible, and comfortable with lying. I loved lying. I made millions lying. No one was better at it. And now I want to say publicly that I regret all the terrible pain and suffering that my lying caused debtors for so many years.[18]

When you pretext for collections, you have to be mean, polite, intelligent, ignorant, or any combination thereof at any given time. Basically, collecting for a living requires the same set of skills required for a man to get into a woman's heavily guarded panties. If you are a man and you disagree with me, then you have not bedded many women who are not hookers. It's okay. Don't worry. I'm sure you're in a happy monogamous relationship with a hot piece of ass

---

17 The *skip* in skip tracing refers to the fact that the target has *skipped* town.
18 See how natural it is for me to lie?

anyway.[19]

All collection agencies assign you an alias. It's like a stripper or actor's stage name. You already met my alias Michael Hart. Michael was a smooth dude who had many different incarnations, jobs, accents, and dialects. He needed to wear a thousand hats because the legitimate collection business had a big disadvantage when compared to Uncle Louie: it was regulated. For example, you were prohibited from calling a debtor before 8am or after 9pm, and—ready for this—you couldn't threaten your debtors. *Imagine that!* I swear I tried to conform to the rules and regulations at first. Then I realized I needed to eat sushi, drive luxury cars, and snort coke in order to survive so I had to figure out ways around these rules.

According to federal law, threatening debtors on the phone falls under unfair and deceptive collection practices. To enforce this regulation, a compliance officer was stationed at all large collection agencies. These assholes—I mean, officers—were parked in the offices to monitor the phones and make sure everyone stayed in line. Did I mention they were assholes? If so, sorry, but I cannot say it enough. Of course, I found ways to work around these assholes; *hey, did I mention these guys were assholes?* As a typical asshole authority figure, they thought everyone liked them. No one ever liked ANY of them, not for one minute. Their job was to get in our way. Fortunately, they all had a penis, which made them easy to manipulate. One guy in particular was a complete dork.[20] Even his mother would say so. Nevertheless, he still actually believed a shower didn't matter and that hot chicks thought he was funny. He loved to drive the ladies crazy by wearing white dress shirts that revealed his dark body hair underneath. Whenever I needed time on the phone to advance a pretext, I would direct one of the cutest office bunnies to hop over and distract the asshole or take him out on a long lunch hour. Sure, my cock-teasing bunnies cost me money—but those rascally rabbits thoroughly enjoyed Operation Distraction whenever called upon for booty duty.

Yet another problem working for a large agency was the geographic scope. You were not just calling debtors in your area. Accounts came onto your desk from all over the country. Although the State of New Jersey where my office was located did not require a collector to be licensed at that time, the majority of states did. This meant that if you were caught not following the collection

---

19 Again, see how natural I sound?
20 Did I mention that this guy was an asshole, too?

laws or a debtor complained to their state Attorney General, you would draw a complaint on behalf of the company. Collection companies were always one of the leading professions when it came to the amount of consumer complaints. To be fair, it's not like the profession is set up to donate toys to kids; it's holding defaulters accountable. Complaints should be expected. Nevertheless, any complaint was a toxic event. When a complaint came in, it didn't matter if the company was fined or sued. One simple complaint would automatically put heat on you as an employee. One too many and you were gone.

In one instance, an overzealous rookie collector still in training attempted to make a name for himself within the company. He was working on the Avon portfolio. Avon sold their skin products and makeup by providing their sales reps and distributors the products upfront. That is correct, I said *upfront*. Naturally, some of their reps sold their products then *forgot* to remit payment for the products to Avon. So every month, low-level JDR collectors chased low-level Avon thieves. This particular rookie was attempting to collect a measly $330 debt for Avon. His actions led to a lawsuit where the Avon sales rep claimed she suffered a miscarriage due to the collector's harassment. No one feels your pain like an American jury and this case was no exception. They awarded her a whooping $800,000. I'll summarize to make sure you understand this legal precedent correctly—she had a fucking miscarriage because someone she stole from turned around and demanded their money back too impolitely. *God Bless America!*

Don't cry for JDR though. With 300 collectors hammering people on the phone all day collecting money, they were able to pay the judgment and keep on trucking. I was one of their best, but I was not satisfied being one out of 300 of anything.

One of kind was what I was after.

SEVEN

IN LESS THAN TWO MONTHS AT JDR, I WENT FROM ROOKIE COLLECTING DELINQUENT $50 Citgo gas cards to being the headliner handling American Express prime accounts. *Prime* meant the account was only 30 days past due. *The fresher the debt, the easier the hunt* held true for several reasons. First, the hunted had not had much time yet to break bad on all their finances. Financial freefall is typically a deliberate process. Second, the hunted did not have much time to disappear off the financial radar so it would be easier to follow their tracks if they tried. Third, the information you did have on them, e.g., employment, residence, bank account, and so on, was still fresh, meaning current. For those reasons, most Amex collection accounts came to my desk fresh.

The problem for American Express from a collection standpoint was they required their cardholders to pay in full within 30 days of the end of the billing cycle. That technically makes them charge cards, not credit cards. Credit cards simply require—and actually prefer—the holder to pay a minimum payment every 30 days (for 30 years). Amex offered no minimum payment options so if their cardholders were delinquent after the 30-day window, swift measures were warranted to ensure they got their money. The longer Amex waited for their money, the less likely a payment in full would result from a collection. Statistics showed that when someone breaks bad financially, they naturally ignore their "payment in full" Amex debt first.

Moreover, American Express corporate culture believed their customers were a high-end clientele. I was the hired gun commissioned when those high-end clients suddenly turned into rear ends. However, to stay true to their corporate image, Amex demanded that even their worst deadbeat clients be treated with the utmost respect and courtesy.[21] Amex felt it had a reputation to uphold even when dealing with scumbags who fucked them over so they selected only certain collectors from approved agencies to work their accounts. Why was I selected? Because I was the best and they didn't drug test. The American Express Company collected a fortune from their asshole high society deadbeat customers, all because of my pretexting scams.

I did so well with the Amex accounts that the bosses at JDR decided to promote me to manager. It didn't last long before I told them I needed to be back in the trenches collecting and skip tracing. The reality was I was not there to move up the company ladder toward a nice house in the suburbs, three kids, and a minivan. I was at JDR to hone my craft, make connections, and learn all the angles that I could exploit to be able to live the real American dream—babes, blow, and limos.

Speaking of babes, JDR offered me an excellent benefits package the owners didn't even know about. I'm not referring to their health and dental plans. Those sucked. I'm talking about their *Friends with Benefits* plan that I was a founding and premium member of. There are many that come to mind, but two in particular stand out, Kristy and Wacky Jackie. They became known as my Spice Girls[22] and they both would help me pave my way to criminal and sexual depravity.

Kristy was about a decade older than I was and the personal assistant to one of the owners of JDR. She took care of his scheduling and was kind enough to provide him an oiled-hand release on a regular basis. There was no contract outlining the terms of her employment. Their arrangement was based solely on a handshake—or *shakes,* in a perverted kind of way. This setup placed Kristy's

---

21 In case it's not abundantly obvious by now, you would much rather owe American Express than Uncle Louie.

22 It was the 90s; give me a break, okay?

expert hands not only on an owner's pulsating lap rocket, but also on the pulse of everything coming and going within JDR. She was no jerk-off either. She literally tugged her way to being the de facto person behind the scenes in charge of divvying out the collection accounts to collection agents. Therefore, I made it my mission in life to earn her trust and I kept her real close once I did. Both during work and after.

Yes, Kristy was a total knockout. But she was also so important that I would have slept with her if she looked and smelled like an orangutan. Lucky for me, she was actually a former Dallas Cowboy cheerleader. Interestingly, she was also a former personal flight assistant to President Clinton... *you already know where this is going, don't you?*

Kristy's favorite hobby was photography, but not taking the pictures; she was into being IN the pictures. She loved to come over to my place and have me photograph her nude. It became my favorite hobby as well. Later on, Kristy made an accusation that President Clinton "groped" her on a flight one time. *I know—what a shocker!* I'm sure if you asked him, he would insist he did not have anything but passenger relations with that woman. Anyway, her revelation made international headlines and thus I got to appear with Kristy on the Howard Stern Show—where brave victims like her and their pimps like me are truly embraced—to display some of the naked pictures from our photo shoots. Kristy sold her story to the Enquirer for $100,000 and I, in turn, sold her naked pictures to an Australian tabloid for $25,000. *Now that was a g'day, mate!*

Besides our twice-weekly film 'n fuck sessions, Kristy proved to be an invaluable mole for me for many years with her deep contacts in Washington—all men who had or wanted to sleep with her or at least get her to stare at their penises. Kristy became my personal "deep throat" (in a couple of ways) and she and her people would eventually assist me in uncovering information on hard-to-find debtors.

Then there was Wacky Jackie. Jackie was another bombshell. Besides her physical beauty, I was attracted to her mind. Before you throw up in your mouth laughing, I was mostly attracted to her body. I said "mind" so that you won't think I am a total pig (yet). Anyway, we met when I was tasked to train her as a collector and it was lust at first sight. Daily training sessions immediately led to nightly ones in bed. Jackie was one of the brightest collectors I knew and she went on to serve many dishonorable years as a distinguished member of my criminal posse. Although Jackie ended up contributing greatly to my felonious future, she did not get busted with me, which probably means she ratted me out. So why did I nickname the brightest collector at JDR Wacky Jackie? I'm pretty sure you can guess that answer by now. If not, keep reading and it will come to you, I promise.

Overall, my *Friends with Benefits* package at JDR was well utilized. I slept with bosses, peers, and subordinates. They came in all shapes, sizes, ages, and fetishes. My *sextracurricular* activities made for some awkward team meetings until I was able to arrange a few group meetings outside the office and inside my bedroom. Turns out, I was great at bringing people together in ways the company never even imagined. *Talk about leadership! And team spirit!* We smoked and drank and fooled around like camp counselors. Kristy and Jackie both had their fun without me. No one had any misconceptions about our arrangement. They were looking for fun and I was young, hung, and always ready to *par-tay!*

One of the best things about JDR was hooking up with my boy, my wingman, Marty. Marty and I sat across from one another at JDR and were a tag-team nightmare if you owed money. We loved pretexting so much that we relentlessly pretexted each other. It kept our skills sharp, I must say.

One morning, Marty picked me up at the service department where I dropped off my car. An hour later, the "service department manager" called to inform me that my Corvette fell off the lift during service. As I totally freaked out on the person on the phone, the entire office was holding back their laughter until they couldn't take it anymore. Marty got me good. But I got him better.

That Friday, on our drive home from work, Marty got pulled over for speeding. As the police officer approached the car, I started staring at Marty with a paranoid look on my face. I then grabbed Marty's knee and screamed out loud just as Johnny Law was at his window, "MARTY, HE'S NOT GONNA CHECK THE FUCKING TRUNK, IS HE?"

It took Johnny Law and his called-in backup a full hour to search the trunk and three days for Marty to start talking to me again.

Being responsible for the American Express prime accounts required that I got the job done by any means necessary without my supervisors or Amex aware of the necessary means I employed. The entire collection industry is commission-based so trying doesn't count, achieving does. There were no awards given out for hardest working employee, longest hours, or best effort. Incidentally, I'm no parent (*thank goodness!*), but I never understood giving all our children trophies for trying. Believe me, you are not doing them any favors rewarding effort. Hard work and effort is nice and all, but the private sector demands results. They don't give a shit about the guy who tries the hardest and fails.[23]

At JDR, if Amex got paid, I got paid, so I made certain they got paid. Thankfully, my bosses passed an unofficial *don't ask, don't tell* policy when it came to how I got the job done. I avoided complaints even though I avoided the rules.

Collecting is a game of cat and mouse, except in my case: I was the cheetah chasing you down. To find you, I did not just zero in on you; I targeted everyone and everything around you. One of the ways I surrounded you was through the use of *nearbys*. Nearbys were my best friends and your worst enemies. All we needed to do was type N-B-Y on our computer keyboard and the system provided the addresses of a debtor's neighbors within 24 hours. It was great tool, especially when targeting people in small towns where everyone knows everyone or in apartment buildings where you could get someone to run upstairs and get the debtor on the phone for you.

This may sound like an unlawful tactic, but it was not unlawful at that time, as long as you did not disclose to the nearby that you were calling about a debt. If you did mention that your call was about a debt, it was flagged as an invasion of privacy and the government considered your call a form of harassment. By the way, the same government does not consider saying "fuck you" to people you legitimately owe money to a form of harassment. *Ain't that fair and balanced!* Therefore when we contacted nearbys, we could only state that it was regarding a *personal matter* and leave them our collector alias and number.

Okay, now for the unlawful part. (You knew it was coming.) By law, you're only supposed to leave a nearby a message like the one mentioned above. I, however, was not a good follower of rules so I would tell the neighbor that I had the debtor's lost wallet or a package from Publishers Clearing House. My intention was to dangle a fat carrot in front of the people who knew my targets in order to retrieve information I sought about my target. My way would always lead to a debtor's phone number or place of work because neighbors, even the

---

23 Of course, if your children go into the public sector, you won't have to worry about any of that.

ones you are not neighborly with, know everything about you. Neighbors know when you come and go. What you do. Who you do it with. Where you work. What your hours are. What you drive. If you don't believe me, *look outside.* There's your neighbor watching you now. Hopefully, he's clothed.

Next was the tax assessor. No one likes the tax assessor. Not even a tax assessor's relatives who live in the same town. If you own a home, you'll find comfort in knowing how many times I used unsuspecting tax assessors in my scams. Once you had a debtor's address, the info on who owns the property was just a phone call away. For example, if I am looking for Jon Stark and I know he lives at 113 Godwin Avenue in North Bergen, New Jersey, I would call the local tax assessor under false pretenses.

"Good morning, this is Michael Hart, an attorney with the FHA in Washington, DC. I need to verify ownership on a piece of property located at 113 Godwin Avenue in North Bergen, New Jersey."

"Did you say 113 Godwin?" the answerer asks, always ready to assist a federal bigwig.

"That's correct," I would say, using my bigwig tone.

"Please hold."

Within two minutes she returns with the ownership information. Now, keep in mind the majority of the time the property doesn't belong to your debtor. Hence, when they give you the name of who actually owns the property, you must also ask for the address the tax bills are being sent to and a phone number if they have one. The secretary at the tax office will sit, roll over, and pee on command for you because you're an attorney from the fucking FHA.

Once you know who owns the property and you know the owner's address, you are ready to contact the landlord, who will definitely know everything about his tenant, your target. The best part about landlords is they are always willing to assist me in cornering you. If you think your neighbors would be helpful to me, think of how helpful your landlord would be. Why? Landlords know everything about you plus they hate you. Only some of your neighbors hate you.[24] All of your landlords do.

Remember: the only reason I am crawling up your ass in the first place is because you're trying to beat someone somewhere for money. That fact tells an expert proctologist like me that your landlord wakes up earlier each morning

---

24 Unless you have a lot of cats; then all of them hate you.

to hate you longer for paying too little, too late, every single fucking month, if anything at all. You probably hate your landlord back, which of course helps me if I'm looking for him. However, most of the time, I'm seeking a tenant target and landlords are always more than happy to load the cannon for me and help me point it right up your ass.

Then there's my military tactic. Some people join the American armed forces to run, jump, fly, and sail in service to their country. Others join to run away from American Express. By tapping into Kristy's military contact down in DC, I was able to find and collect debts from more than a few good men. I became very familiar with APO and FPO, which are the military addresses for stationed personnel.[25]

Using my target's name, date of birth, and social security number, I was able to obtain their military location and commanding officer's information. So what did I do with that information? I certainly didn't call my debtor. Instead, I called his commanding officer to notify them of the GI who took advantage of me and owes me money. One thing the military hates is skirting financial responsibilities. And one thing commanding officers hate is to be bothered by anything at all so they would routinely tell my debtors about my call and give a direct or indirect order to take care of it. From there, I would get a call from GI Joe Schmoe who would tell me that he will take care of the matter immediately. *Two words, Soldier: Western Union!* You can access it anywhere on the Western Front!

To all the commanding officers over the years who have assisted me in collecting my money, I salute you. *Fire!*

I also created unique skip tracing tactics to develop contacts via a target's credit report. Being designated an agent of the OC (original creditor), you inherit the legal authority to pull a credit report on someone as long as you indicate "any information used is in an attempt to collect a debt."[26]

---

25 The difference between the "A" and "F" before the "PO" is domestic and international.

26 One of my fellow crazy collectors at JDR boldly tested the reach of this regulation by attempting to pull a report on President George W. Bush, using no social security number and the address of the White House. Although no information showed up on the screen, the Secret Service showed up at the office the next day. The real shocker was that the collector wasn't fired. He was merely reprimanded. Probably because management saw that he had balls, and balls—especially elephant balls like mine— bred success in the collection business.

Once I had a debtor's credit report, I went to work like a surgeon. A credit report provides past and current addresses as well as past and current employment information. It lists all reportable debts, liens, loans, and mortgages. Basically, you get to review all of your competition for your target deadbeat's money. For example, if you see they are paying Honda Credit, you know it's a car loan or lease payment. I would then call Honda directly and ask for the skip tracing department.

Skip tracing departments are at every major bank and finance company. They extend courtesy about credit worthiness to other banks and finance companies because they need one another. *Big Brother never stops watching you in the Land of the Free!* The authority of the skip tracing department is found in the small print you never read buried in the loan documents you sign: "Should the applicant ever become delinquent, you hereby authorize the bank to exchange information on you with other financial institutions." This clause has two purposes. One, it allows them to sell your information on promotional lists to other banks. Two, it helps them disclose you as a deadbeat should you ever stop paying on the account so everyone can gang bang you.

Having insider contacts and piercing banks for information is eventually what got me into this mess, but it is the backbone of being successful in the collection business. With a direct line to a contact at a financial institution, you can call them and get right down to business, "Hi, this is Ozzy for JDR, I need help on a skip. John Debtor Doe, his social is 123-45-6789." Since you both have them in your databases, your contact will provide information they have, which may be different than what you have. You then compare information and notes on the target, which is all perfectly legal per the small print.

The best contacts for skip tracing, by far, are auto finance companies. Collectors all recognize that auto finance companies have the biggest swinging cocks in the industry and to be successful you have to be able to tap into their information. Why? Because if you stop paying on a credit card, you can always tell my client American Express to go fuck themselves, which was not uncommon. But if you stop paying your car note, they repossess it in the middle of the night and you have to take the bus. *Fuck who?*

My contacts grew exponentially until I covered most banks from Amalgamated to Zales. If I did not have a contact, I would reach out while impersonating Jack Mazzola, a childhood friend who now worked at GMAC, the nation's leading auto finance company. He was a real bigwig and had no idea I was making calls as him. I bet I made more calls as him on some days than he did as him. Impersonation always yielded the best cooperation. Cooperation always produced helpful information. What if I had played by the rules? Then I would still be trying to locate my first target.

My unconventional methods brought unconventional success rates. Everyone knew I was bending rules or maybe even breaking them into a million pieces. Regardless, JDR's bigger clients took notice of who was delivering the biggest babies in the company and before long I started doing collection and skip trace work on the side for them. However, a lot of my side business came from my PI contacts that relied on me and paid me for information they could not retrieve because... well... they wouldn't break the law themselves, but they would pay for me to do it. Non-published phone numbers and credit reports are gold to private investigators. Credit reports were by far the biggest moneymaker. If husbands are cheating or trying to hide assets for a divorce, a credit report tells you everything that is going on with them financially.

The problem for PIs was that they did not have direct access to credit reports and they left dinosaur footprints whenever they had someone else pull the report for them in the form of an inquiry. A credit inquiry is time-and-date stamped by the credit reporting agency and remains on the report for up to two years. To make matters worse for snoops, a subject under investigation can easily be tipped off by looking at their personal report. If the company that did the actual pulling of the report did not have a permissible purpose to do so, then the law imposed the risk of huge fines. But their new best friend Ozzy was undetectable in his methods. No footprints. Problem solved.

This is where Kristy comes in again. She was now my most valuable player, in and out of bed. She became friendly with the girls at the credit reporting agencies and was able to call them and actually have an inquiry removed *before* anyone was notified. You know—just a little girl talk sprinkled with a little invasion of privacy. We received the actual report and left no inquiry trace in doing so!

Kristy's contact girls, not making the big bucks at their jobs,[27] were thrilled to receive gift cards at their homes from random strangers. During company

---

27 The underpaid always present a great opportunity to exploit, and every American, including welfare recipients and corporate bigwigs, believes they are underpaid.

time, I was selling hundreds of credit reports for a hundred bucks each. It took 30 seconds to run one and cover it like it never happened. Kristy got her 20% cut. Her co-conspirators went shopping for new shoes and handbags. Nails got done. Highlights were added. New jewelry sparkled.

And jilted wives everywhere got their marital revenge.

EIGHT

WHEN YOU HAVE THE BEST COCAINE, THERE'S NO NEED TO ADVERTISE. Users come to you. Similarly, word spread throughout the private investigation world about my uniquely effective services like wildfire. I was the only game in town doing it. No one knew how I was doing it and no one tried to duplicate my duplicity. Dozens of PIs literally knocked on my home door (that's what PIs do when they want to speak to you), trying to get in with me. I enticed them with credit reports, then sold them on a whole range of other valuable services they needed, i.e., information brokering. They were then billing their clients outrageous fees for the work I was doing for them.

Here's where Jackie comes in. Besides working at JDR during the day, Jackie worked for a company called Investicorp at night—I told you she was bright. Investicorp was a licensed private investigation firm that specialized in two services. One was secret employees. They placed workers inside large companies where no one, except perhaps a security officer or owner, knew the real reason they were there. The spy employee provided reports to Investicorp regarding who was stealing, not working, sleeping together, selling drugs, using drugs, etc.[28]

Investicorp got paid handsomely to deliver insider knowledge of all corporate wrongdoings. The average employee-spying stint would last anywhere from three months to a year. The great thing for the secret employee is that they were allowed to keep both of the paychecks, the one from Investicorp and the one from the company they were investigating. One night during after-sex talk, Jackie confessed to me that she was placed inside JDR by potential investors who were planning on purchasing the agency and wanted a complete report as to what was going on throughout the company.

Investicorp, she explained, was run by two sisters, Rose and Judy. Judy took care of the undercover employee arm of the business, whereas Rose ran the domestic end of the business, which primarily reported on husband, wife, boyfriend, or girlfriend infidelity. Jackie was a double agent in multiple ways as Investicorp utilized her assets (and ass) for both arms of their business. She was being paid to moonlight and being paid to lure suspected cheating men out of bars and into predetermined locations like a hotel room or restaurant and get it captured on audio or video. I want to go on record and say this was not a fair set-up in my opinion. Seriously, what man had the willpower to resist Jackie in a low-cut blouse and short skirt? Even if he never cheated before in his life, he had no choice but to now. Pointing a gun to his head would be fairer.

Now you see why Jackie was bright, ambitious, and wacky. Wait. Are you still confused about the wacky part? Let me clear that up—she was a violent sex animal. Jackie loved to be whacked and whack me back. Giving her booze and drugs was like going over to Hannibal Lecter's house wearing raspberry vinaigrette cologne. She was downright nasty. And I loved her for it. There was so much biting, hitting, and trash talk going on during sex that it sounded like a Jerry Springer episode in my bedroom without the beeps.

One crazy night, I ungagged her and she screamed, "Hit me! Hit me!" I tried slapping her in the face just to calm her down but she just smiled demonically and yelled, "Do it again! Harder, you fuckin' pussy!" *Wow, that backfired!* I was hoping my neighbors would call the police. Or a priest. I would not have been surprised if her head started doing 360s before she hurled pea soup all over my bedroom. So I did what any reasonable person concerned for their own safety

---

28 Of course, I was personally engaged in all those activities at JDR. Luckily, I was also banging the spy on regular rotation.

would do—I videotaped our sessions so I could watch them over and over again while I masturbated. To this day, never in my life have I ever been so scared and turned on by one woman at the same time. The best part was the next morning was like an exorcism took place and Jackie's memory had been erased. She never talked about or even mentioned what had transpired the night before. It was like we had a pleasant, quiet evening playing Scrabble and drinking cocoa instead of engaging in mixed marital arts sexual combat inside the octagon.

Since Jackie and I worked together and played together, like Frazier and Ali, it was now time to take our business relationship to the next level. Jackie worked at Investicorp for two purposes: the dual paycheck she was getting, plus she was in an apprenticeship to become a fully licensed private investigator.

The process of getting licensed consisted of a two-year apprenticeship working under a licensed PI and then passing a state-mandated test issued by the state police. You also had to pass a background check. In order to do what I was planning to do next, I needed that license.

Then I thought about it. *Hmmm*...a license would bring more regulation and more scrutiny to my methods. I preferred to operate in the shadows, like Batman. What I decided I needed was *access* to someone with that license. And maybe that someone could be Jackie...

One fateful day, Jackie got an urgent call from her boss Rose at Investicorp. They were working for a very wealthy client and needed information right away. Apparently, this mega-rich client was planning on marrying a guy who was suspect in the faithful arena, (but what guy isn't?) which made him Investicorp's target. When the wealthy fiancé found out that her potentially cheating sweetheart was going on a spur-of-the-moment business trip to Florida, she suspected he was meeting another lady. Problem was the suspect was already airborne.

One of Rose's investigators had tailed him to the airport and saw he was flying into Fort Lauderdale so the investigator hopped on the next flight to Fort Lauderdale and hoped for a miracle as he was far behind his target and had no hope of catching up to him once he landed without solid reconnaissance. Unless, somehow, he got an address or lead on the mystery woman, the tail was a waste of time. Rose told Jackie that she needed an address immediately and was willing to pay top dollar to get it.

Jackie flashed me the bat signal because I was the best and I lived for moments like this. Pretexting demanded a killer instinct under intense time constraints. Fail and earn nothing. Succeed and earn big. All I had was the suspect's name, his home telephone number, and a pretty good idea the female subject resided somewhere in Florida. I immediately called New Jersey Bell posing as a regional supervisor for Southern Bell, located in Pensacola, Florida. The pretext to NJ Bell was I worked for their sister company in Florida and was investigating a customer who was challenging their bill—basically denying making certain calls and attempting to get a credit on their bill for said calls. In those instances, the phone company that services the number in question does what is called check-for-returns. Being affiliated "dumb" Bells, the two companies shared common codes so they cooperated completely with my completely unethical request. Remember, these were the days before unlimited calling plans and it cost a few bucks to call Florida and all calls were itemized on your monthly bill.

The New Jersey dumbbell gladly pulled my cheater's last two monthly bills to provide me with *proof of conversation*. She informed me of two specific Florida phone numbers and varying lengths of calls ranging from five minutes up to two hours at all different times of day and night. The numbers were a Fort Lauderdale exchange. *Now isn't that nice!*

Next step was to contact the Southern Bell CNA department.[29] Remember fellow thieves—know your lingo and terminology, especially when you are operating under false pretenses. CNA was an internal phone company department that was critical in the commission of thousands of my scams. Why? They verified phone numbers if you provided them with proper corresponding codes for your request. For example, if a customer in California had a New Jersey telephone number on their phone bill that they did not recognize, they would call Pacific Bell, their local phone company in California. To assist their customer, Pacific Bell would call New Jersey Bell's CNA Department to verify the New Jersey phone number. If you think I was waiting on hold like the rest of you, think again. The phone numbers for CNA Departments are all internal, so unlike you, I get right through.

"CNA Department, this is Debbie speaking. How may I help you?"

My lying begins. "Good afternoon Debbie. This is Michael Hart with AT&T and my code is 1-1-1." That was the actual legitimate code I obtained <u>and utilized illegitimately</u> back then.

29 CNA stands for Customer Name Address.

After checking my code for clearance, she tells me, "Go ahead, Michael."

"I have two listings for you, 305-427-3969 and 305-423-4277." These are numbers I got from the Jersey dumbbell.

She types them in and *bingo!* "The first listing is residential to a Sandra Piscopo. The address is residential located at 125 Yardley Avenue, Apartment 4A, in Fort Lauderdale." *Got it, go on.* "The second number is a business, Jazz Salon, located at 1013 Rock Road, and also in Fort Lauderdale." *Thank you and goodbye.*

The first number I dialed was the home number for Sandra. After three rings, there she was, with her sultry, mistress voice: "Hi, this is Sandra, please leave a message and I will call you back." *Beeeeep.*

I was so aroused I wanted to leave her a singing message—*Oh, Sandy, can't you see I'm in misery*—but time was of the essence so I hung up, picked right back up, and dialed the Jazz Salon number. This time a live person answers, young and sweet-sounding herself, but different from Sandra's sultry voice. "Thank you for calling Jazz Salon. May I help you?"

"Hi. Is Sandra in?" I inquire.

"She's with a client right now. May I help you with something?"

"No, thanks. I'll call back later."

Bada-Bing-Bada-Boom-Boom-Boom-Bitches! I danced my way over to Jackie's cubicle, tapped her on the shoulder and dropped my notes containing the phone numbers, name, and place of employment for the previously unknown subject. Less than 30 minutes had elapsed since the bat signal went up and the Joker was located. Jackie was completely amazed, which meant I was in for a hurting that night. She called Rose immediately who was even more amazed.

Rose relayed the information to her local investigator as soon as he landed in Fort Lauderdale. A few hours later, the investigator spotted the targets together at the Jazz Salon. He snapped photos and recorded videos as they left and followed them to their love hideaway where they frolicked for hours. I recall saying to myself back then, *this poor fucking guy just wanted to get laid before his wedding and instead he got royally fucked. Riddle me that, Batman!*

✦ ■ ✦

Rose told Jackie she wanted to meet the great wizard Ozzy in person to pay me for my services. And I wanted to meet her for a million business reasons. I could tell Jackie wasn't exactly thrilled about not being invited to our meet-up, but business comes first. A week later, Rose and I met at Houston's at the Riverside Square Mall in Hackensack. Rose was a delightfully thin and attractive older woman, not that I was real picky.

We enjoyed dinner with a bottle of wine. Then another. Then another. Then one more. During dinner, we discussed deepening our business relationship. I also listened to how boring married life was for her and got the sense that Jackie may have had a little girl talk about me with Rose. I made a mental note.

Rose was so impressed by my bag of magic tricks that she said she already gave my number to her other contacts. I asked her if there was a way for me to work under her license for the two-year apprenticeship so that I could get my PI license, like Jackie. I didn't tell her I wasn't really interested in the license and I just wanted to learn everything I could about private investigation and expand my connections. At that moment, Rose had finished her umpteenth glass of wine with one last gulp before she responded. "I *could* have you do that… but you're going to have to do something for me then. I'm just not sure what that *could* be—"

Now I've watched enough Animal Planet to realize how cougars communicate to the young cubs, so I looked at my watch and saw what time it was. Time to go in for the kill. "Well, why don't we go back to my place and discuss it there?" After all, her place had a husband, a couple of kids, and a Cockapoo.

"Let's go," she instantly replied.

"Check, please!"

The drive from where we were in Hackensack to my condo in Hawthorne takes fifteen minutes. I made it in seven. As soon as we walked through my door, Rose did not stop after she removed her coat. She kept removing her clothes as we headed straight to my bedroom. I always lived by the adage desire wasn't put in your pants to stay. Desire is not desire, until you give it away, especially to a married woman with a Cockapoo. The irony that her firm was in business to catch people like her doing what we were doing was also a great aphrodisiac.

I pushed Rose onto my bed. I did not go down on her. I went up—starting from her toes using my hands and tongue…then slowly up each of her smooth legs, eventually burying my face on her dripping wet, hairless pussy. I could tell this was what she wanted (so did I) when she wrapped her legs around my head so tightly my eyeballs almost popped out of my skull. I stayed there for multiple, gyrating, intense, screaming orgasms before I tagged in Little Ozzy to finish her off.

Two hours later, Little Ozzy and I emerged from the bedroom sweaty, sticky, satisfied, and with something that all Italians strive for, a no-show job.

The agreement we christened— many times over—was for me to be put "on the books" at Investicorp earning my state-mandated time for licensing requirements and learning the ropes. In exchange, I would provide Rose discounted skip trace services and information and likely (hopefully) some more favors of the flesh. *Hey, don't judge!* Women are entitled to sleep their way to the top, so shouldn't I be entitled to sleep my way to the bottom?

Between Kristy, Rose, and Jackie, I was barely getting any sleep. Insomnia doesn't suck for everyone. My relationship with Rose blossomed financially and sexually. Sexually, I must say, it got a little creepy between us when, one time in bed after another orally-induced orgasm from me, she turned over and asked me if I would consider marrying her twenty-year-old daughter.

Wha…wha…what the fuck did she just say?

There are very few statements that can shock a professional shocker. But there I was—still shiny-faced with her sex nectar—totally dumbfounded. For the first time in my life, I was without words. *Is she kidding? Do I laugh? Should I cry? Is this another demonic possession? Should I wipe my chin..?*

Before I could craft a response, Rose upped the creepiness, stating matter-of-factly, "I know she's Jewish, but I really think you two would make a great couple…" I laughed it off on the outside but I was freaking out inside my head. Suddenly, the freaky head inside my underpants thought it through and started to swell again. So I fucked her until we both climaxed. *Holy mother-in-lawless!*

NINE

FROM THE DAY I BEGAN WORKING THERE, I WAS PLOTTING MY EXIT FROM JDR. After about two years, there was nothing left for me to learn at JDR. I had perfected all my tricks (and treats) on their dime, made a few bucks, established valuable connections, partied hearty with Marty, and slept with everyone I should and shouldn't have.

Don't think my tenure didn't benefit the shareholders of JDR. They made a financial killing off of my work and the work of my team. How well did they do? Well—a few years later JDR was purchased by NCO Financial, which was the largest collection agency in the country for somewhere in the area of $240 million. Jackie was their mole. You can say we all used each other and all ended up better off.

The next stop for the Lembo Crazy Train was to launch my own operation in information brokering. To do that, I needed to get my hands on a couple hundred grand in start-up capital. The good news was I had a steady cash flow from my side work that was growing. The bad news was my *cash blow* was happening faster. Two hundred grand was not to be found stuffed inside my mattress (yet), although it may well have been snuffed up by my nose by then.

No bank was interested in me either. No bank was ever interested in me, which was kind of unfair considering I was charged later on for being so interested in them. That left me no choice but to ask my best friend in the whole world to get me the cash. Mr. Michael Hart.

Michael Hart was more than just an alias; he was an actual separate person, at least as far as the rest of the world was concerned. It should be obvious by now that I seriously considered naming my alias Michael Hunt instead, but ultimately settled on Hart.[30]

Until now, no one ever knew that Michael Hart was a complete mirage all along. Like Dr. Frankenstein, I gave him life and then cultivated him for bad intentions. Then his intentions only got worse. It happens. Like all hoods, Michael Hart started out small. In the early 90s, compact discs were booming. A company called Columbia House offered twelve CDs for one cent if you became a member. The deal was you had to buy a minimum of five more at regular price. If you did that, you were done with the membership and had 17 rockin' new CDs.

Michael Hart, who lived with me at my condo, loved music, so he joined Columbia House's promotion. Companies such as Columbia House sold their paid-in-full, preferred customer lists to other companies so, sure enough, pre-approved offers of credit started flooding in for my completely made-up roommate. Within a few months, Michael had several credit cards with an average credit limit of $5,000 per.

Michael may have not existed, but he was nonetheless a savvy son-of-a-bitch. He knew the inside rules for all credit cards:

1. Pay your bills on time.
2. Do not go over 49% of your credit limit.
3. Never issue a bad check.
4. Do the above for at least six months.

Michael was a very patient imaginary man who played by the rules and earned a triple credit rating attached to his newly-found social security number created using the exact parameters for the state he was born in and the time he was born.[31] Accordingly, his credit limits increased. Everything was illegal and

---

30 If you don't know why I decided to go with Hart over Hunt, you're going to have to ask someone.

31 Told ya he was a savvy son-of-a-bitch.

on the up-and-up at the same time.

Michael's roommate, Ozzy, conveniently worked for cash. Ozzy was also kind enough to write money orders for Michael to pay all his bills every month. Michael was extremely conscientious when it came to his fraudulent finances and kept all his bills up to date every month.

Six months was the minimum time frame to keep credit cards out of fraud detection. Thus, a day after six months passed on the calendar, Ozzy asked Michael to help him finance his new startup. Michael was the quiet type, but very generous to his only friend. With very little persuasion, Michael agreed to help his friend fulfill his dream. *Isn't that what imaginary friends are for?*

They sat down and put together a plan. The plan was for Michael to go bad. Real fucking bad, real fucking fast.

Michael went from playing by the rules over the course of several months to maxing out all his credit cards by making major purchases and taking huge cash advances in a matter of a few days. Of course, when the bills came, it would be illegal for Michael's roommate Ozzy to write bad checks, so they decided to put those decorative credit card checks to good use. Discover checks paid the Citibank account in full, bringing Citi card down to a zero balance because Michael Hart did not have a bad check history. Chase checks paid the American Express in full, bringing Amex down to zero balance. And so on. Michael did this knowing that his multiple credit lines were now maxed out and those cute little checks would eventually be returned back for "unavailable credit." *Oops!*

Why all the shuffling? Well, it takes the bank at least a week to return those silly little checks back to Michael, so during that time frame Michael has the opportunity to max out each card once again. Before you start writing checks and maxing out your credit cards twice over, be advised that people like me and scenarios like this have changed the game. I know and I'm sorry.[32] You'll just have to come up with your own scheme to defraud.

In any event, you have to admit Michael was a generous figment of my imagination. When the dust settled, he'd maxed out several cards, twice, for about $10,000 each. Even better, the actions taken by Michael were *civil* in nature, not criminal. *What happened?* Michael just lost control of his finances. It happens every day. Turns out, it even happens to ghosts.[33]

---

32 Once again, see how natural I sound?
33 Oh yeah—I forgot to mention that identity theft had yet to become the booming crime it would. Michael Hart was truly a trendsetter.

But just when you thought he'd fallen far enough, Michael fell further. He was never satisfied so he tried another round on his credit experiment. *What balls! What talent!* The remarkable part was some card companies actually fell for it once again. These dipshits were begging to be taught a lesson. In total, Michael took $224,000 in cash advances and merchandise from his creditors and donated every penny to his creator, Dr. Oz, just before he vanished into thin air. *What a friendly ghost!*

Because he left without even saying goodbye, I had no idea where he was and had to have his mail returned to sender via the US Postal Service as "moved; left no forwarding address." Any time a call came in for him, I immediately went ballistic. "Michael Hart! That mother fuckin' lowlife scumbag! He was my roommate and moved out in the middle of the night owing me thousands. He also fucked my girlfriend and took my rollerblades so when you find that asshole, tell him to call ME!"[34]

About a decade after my ingenious Michael Hart scam, identity theft really started to take off. However, the tactics never really made sense to me. Why would you steal someone's information when you could simply make a person up? If you steal someone's identity, a complaint is filed the minute the victim finds out and a civil and/or criminal investigation is commenced. To me, traditional identity theft leaves a risky trail of scorned victims and paper. The Michael Hart way of wrongdoing had no angry victims. Sure, over time credit card companies would lose a little off their billion-dollar bottom line, but likely not enough to compel them to go after a ghost who completely scammed them and risk having the world find out. *Boo!*

At the age of 21, my formal education was done. I completed my requisite courses in Uncle Louie, JDR, Investicorp, and Michael Hart and proudly received all the dishonors and privileges that my street degree in criminal law conferred upon me. I was equally proud of earning a dual minor in sex education and toxicology. Combining my degrees and stolen startup money, I opened DRL Associates. Like Godzilla on Tokyo, my reign of terror on debtors

---

34 A few years later after I moved, I received a call from an "old friend" of Michael Hart's claiming to be in town and trying to reach him. I asked what for and the caller told me he had tickets to the Yankee game for that weekend and wanted to get together. I hired him on the spot.

was unleashed.

DRL was a full-service collection agency and totally legitimate to an unsuspecting eye. Rose and I had switched positions many times inside the bedroom and now we switched positions outside of it as she started working for me. My corporate slogan was "Diversification in Information" which meant, "We do whatever the fuck is necessary to get your job done!"

It was 1992, and the times, they were a-changing. Technology started to revolutionize the collection business. The internet was just a fetus. Cell phones would soon be in everyone's hands. Credit laws were also changing dramatically. Collectors were no longer able to simply pick up the phone and call debtors, over and over again, and wear them down into submission. Most significantly, Caller ID and Call Block would soon prevent people like me from performing my dirty tricks in traditional fashion.

To make matters worse, the RICO Act[35] was now increasingly used by prosecutors in deterring bad guys like me. Its original target was to break the balls, back, and bank of the mob, which it did. Unfortunately, my being ejected from the mob at an early age didn't spare me RICO exposure. The RICO statute scared every racketeer, and rightfully so. It was designed to dry-fuck us all up the ass with no grease wearing a sandpaper condom. Not only was it easy to prove, the penalties—fines, prison time, and seizures—were crushing. Simply directing someone to knock on a debtor's door and demand money they owed you could have you facing 20 fucking years. *Ouch!*

Luckily, violence was not part of my business model or the government would have brought me down in minutes, not the more than a decade it took them. Truthfully, violence was rarely necessary in my business. Nor was violence a strategy I implemented often in my fucked-up personal life. Not that I was above it; it was simply too risky in my line of work. Sure, there were times where I had to kick some ass—or have my people do it so I didn't scuff my expensive Italian leather shoes—but those times were way fewer than you would expect given my life of crime and associations. In fact, considering the dastardly deeds I was engaged in for years and the company I kept, it is hard

---

35 The RICO Act (Racketeer Influenced and Corrupt Organizations Act) focuses specifically on racketeering, and it allows for the *leaders* of a syndicate to be tried for the crimes which they ordered others to do or assisted them, thus closing a loophole that allowed someone who told a man to, for example, murder, to be exempt from the trial because he did not commit the crime personally.

for me to fathom how I was able to survive, let alone thrive, almost exclusively with my brains. And penis. And cocaine.

I advertised and branded DRL as the driving force of information all over the east coast. My chop shop (read: *office*) was set up in a high-end condo located in the Ritz Plaza in Hackensack. No decorating expense was spared. I ran a top-shelf, first-class corrupt enterprise. The people who worked for me were selected and trained by me personally in reverse collections, pretexting, etc. As a constant reminder, I hung a sign over their computers that read "WWOD", which stood for *What Would Ozzy Do?* The answer was usually the opposite of what would Jesus do.

There was no asshole compliance officer monitoring our phones. No one was there to make sure we were following burdensome collection laws. In fact, the only person checking up on you was me. And I was there only to make sure you were delivering, no matter how. I trained my minions on what to do, when to do it, and what not to do. I expected results or I cut you loose. My professional peeps needed to know how to disguise and improvise—sing, dance, and bake a chocolate cake, if necessary. Debtors are seasoned professionals themselves. They knew the tricks and had a lot of them up their sleeves also. Remember, anyone can get into debt (and it seemed like everyone did.) Only a true professional deadbeat can hide forever from it.

In the end, only a select few employees had big enough balls to work for me. Fewer still were able to stay on for the long haul. Loyalty was essential. So was no complaining. I demanded fearlessness. Ferociousness. Precociousness. Only our targets were allowed to cry. *Don't tell me about how long your hours are. Deliver! Don't tell me how difficult the pregnancy is. Just show me the bloody baby!* Do that—and I'll pay you more than you could ever make legitimately.

Thick skin was required and not just to withstand dealing with unstable, explosive debtors on a daily basis. You needed it to endure your unstable, explosive boss who would harass you inappropriately whether he was in a good mood or bad mood. But sexual harassment wasn't a problem for the women who worked for me. I fucked them all *before* I hired them. I fucked most of them *during* their time of employment. And I fucked some of them *after* they left. But in the end, some of them ended up fucking me behind my back.

TEN

AT DRL, WE SAID WHAT WE MEANT AND DID WHAT WE SAID. We prided ourselves on our reputation of solving problems by any means necessary. One day, I got a call from an accountant named Peter. Peter had a big problem and had heard from a mutual friend that I was a fixer. He had prepared a tax return for a client and the client bounced a $5,000 check to him. Peter wasn't a major corporation or large business. He was a small business owner, a local CPA, and that amount of money made a big difference to his bottom line. Peter tried everything he could, from calling the client to sending him letters. No luck. The letters were returned by the post office stamped "moved; left no forwarding address."[36]

When Peter came in, he was understandably distraught. The matter was personal to him. I listened to him bitch and moan for a couple of minutes and then cut him off by telling him I could solve his problem but my fee was 50% of the collected amount. Without hesitation, Peter agreed, pulled the bounced

---

36 No, the client was not Michael Hart. Good question, though!

check from his briefcase, and handed it to me. What other choice did he have? One hundred percent of zero was his only other choice.

Right away I noticed the check was stamped "NSF" for "non-sufficient funds." It was drawn on a Valley National Bank account. The check number was 813. Finally, I saw the check was not hole-punched and it was made payable to Peter Yurkowski. All were critical clues to a wizard of crime:

1.   The high check number indicated the account had likely been open for a while.
2.   The "NSF" stamp on the front indicated the account was still open.
3.   The fact that the check was not hole-punched meant it had only been deposited once and not twice.

After Peter left, I called my contact at that particular bank and gave her the account number for the check. She readily (and unlawfully) informed me that the account had not had a $5,000 balance for over a year. Not good news. The account was then entered into our database and categorized under collection rotation with notes attached reading "target never answers the phone" and "no address". My runners searched his last-known neighborhood for information on the check bouncer's new residence. No luck. Maybe this guy was traveling into oblivion with Mr. Hart. Or maybe not. Daily, for about a month, we verified funds in his bank account through my contact. Still no luck. Then one morning, the case broke. I got a call from my bank contact monitoring his account. She told me he now had $4,780 in it! It was a little short of pay dirt, but damn close enough. To the phones…

"Peter, it's Ozzy. Quick question: do you have a picture on your driver's license?"

"Yeah—why?"

I had no time for discussion. "Good. Be at my office in an hour."

An hour later, I had Peter's driver's license in my hand and a look of confusion on his face. I looked at the picture and concluded it was close enough. "Relax," I told him. "Have a drink. Take a nap. Hit the bong. Flirt with the girls. I'll be back in an hour."

Leaving Peter at my office, I raced over to the nearest Valley National location, went inside, and grabbed a deposit slip. Back in my car I filled out the cash deposit slip in the amount of $221 with our target's corresponding account number. At the drive thru window, I handed my deposit slip with the stated amount of cash (which was my cash) over to the teller at the window and asked her, "Will this post right away?"

"Cash always does," she replied. *Thank you!* [37]

The next trick was always prohibited for obvious reasons but I still did it for obvious reasons. Ten minutes later, I walked into a different location of Valley National Bank, wearing my hair up in my trusty old Fordham baseball cap. I got on line and waited my turn. At the call of my turn, I stepped up to the teller's window and told her my client had just informed me the money for the returned check he wrote me was now available in his account. With the check in her one hand, she punched up the account information with the other. She looked at the check again, then verified the amount and said, "Mr. Yurkowski, do you have any identification?"

"I think so," I responded while pretending to search through my wallet. "Ah, here it is," I said, handing it over to her.

After a short glimpse of the license, the cute teller turned to me and said. "You look much younger in person."

With a bashful smile on my face, I replied, "I've started using face cream."

She smirked and asked "How would you like that?"

"All hundreds, please."

A half-hour later, I walked back into my office and handed Peter 2,500 in cash. He was so appreciative we became lifelong friends and he invited me to all three of his weddings.

When the internet craze kicked off, information became more plentiful and accessible. Information was my commodity. I sold it, traded it, bartered it, and even created it when I had to. The difference was I was a merchant of private information, and, in some cases, privileged information. Did you ever hear of a guy who knows a guy that is friends with a guy who can get you any type of information? Well, I was that guy. If you needed information, you just needed to find me. I would find the rest. For a hefty price.

Welcome! Come into my office, sit down, have a drink, perhaps a pinch of coke, if that's your thing. Now tell your Uncle Ozzy what is troubling you. What is it that you need in your life that you don't have?

---

37 Cash posts to your account immediately because it doesn't require any overnight processing and doesn't need to clear. *It's cash, baby!* Again, this is another trick that would be prohibited by banks today. So again—I'm sorry. *(see footnotes 18, 19, 32)*

I had access to it all. Cell phone bills. Home phone bills. Home addresses of long-lost loves. Birth parents. Children put up for adoption. Receivables. Credit reports. Bank records. Medical records. Driving records. Marriage records. Sealed court files. Evictions. Child support. Unpublished phone numbers. Bad checks. Criminal records. Judgments. Anything that was not in the public domain was in my domain, readily accessible, and available through my covert network of payoffs and schemes. Dirty deeds, not done dirt cheap.

Who were the type of people who came in to see me? Many were professionals. Some were not. Some were just like you. Some probably were you. Some were probably looking for you. I had all kinds of clients, like private investigators, lawyers, cops, wiseguys, divorcees, parents, employers, employees, landlords, tenants, your neighbors, and law enforcement personnel. All were basically good people who were wronged and they were after the bad people who wronged them. The yellow brick road leading to The Dark Wizard of Oz was getting more crowded by the day. Just remember that when you speak to the wizard, don't ask him how he obtained the information you are seeking. Don't ask him or any of his Munchkins how he runs his business or what they do after hours. We ain't in Kansas. This is Hacken-fucking-sack, New Jersey. How dare you question the wizard? The grand wizard answers to no one—especially those who ask questions an undercover fed would ask in an attempt to set him up.

If you make the grave mistake of asking about how I do my business— sorry, Dorothy, but the wizard won't help you. Have a nice day. By the way, nice shoes. You pay my firm for results and only results, not for our policies or procedures. And most definitely not for our ethics. Our immoral operation was morally justifiable to our clients because most every one of them came to us only after being swindled by our targets. Information Vigilantism, Incorporated.

Cops, in particular, loved to gather information on certain people, especially pertaining to wives and girlfriends. It was professional suicide for them to risk utilizing the vast law enforcement databases for unethical or unlawful purposes. Getting caught meant severe discipline and, in some cases, possibly burning your badge. Unlike the laws in the Land of Oz, the laws of our great country require you first have just cause to investigate a suspect.[38] And even

38 Apparently, this is what the founding fathers wrote into the Constitution. I'm certain they did this because each of them had a stable of mistresses they were hiding from the founding mothers.

with just cause, you must follow proper procedures and document everything. The Constitution does not recognize your jilted penis as an acceptable legal justification for conducting a search into another American.

We represented thousands of penises and vaginas. So when a cop wanted to learn about the driving record of the legitimate boyfriend standing in the way of his illegitimate affair, he turned to me. And turned the other way on all the drugs I was consuming. *Quid pro blow*.

In some cases, I actually paid cops to run searches against individuals that another cop wanted but could not do himself because they were too close to the fire. *What a great fucked up country!*

A lesson for you: *Never let a bill collector get inside your head*. It's like inviting a vampire into your home. Once invited in, you are rendered powerless and soon-to-be wallet-less. Once you opened the door—even if only an inch—we kicked the door down and mind-fucked you until you paid us to spare your neck and move on. My stable of ruthless vampires knew how to suck the life out of you and your family. They were experts at mind-fucking you and dominating your thoughts until you submitted to our charade. You were with left with no choice but to submit to us… and you could make it easy on yourself or hard.

"Hello, this is Michael Hart. Is this Marie Russo?" *Know your debtor because they all have an angle you can exploit.* I've done my homework and know this deadbeat is confrontational so I'm assertive from hello.

"Yes, it is." I can tell by her tone that her attitude is already out and about. *Excellent.*

"Ms. Russo, what seems to be the problem here? My employee is trying to get you to live up to your obligation for a medical bill and you are being rude and abrasive toward him for doing his job." This is the bad cop/worse cop scenario for collections. Basically, we are trying to obtain employment information for Ms. Russo. She owes a $419 bill to a dentist who is now my client. My employee set her up; I am called in to close the deal.

"His job?" she declares. "That employee of yours keeps threatening me that he is going to do this or do that if I don't pay." I don't respond; she is on a roll. "Now you listen to me carefully, Mr. Hart. I didn't put up with threats from my ex-husband and I am certainly not going to put up with threats from you, your employee, or any man!" She is burning mad. But she has not hung up. She likes to fight. She wants to fight. And I always give a lady what she wants.

"Ms. Russo, that attitude is exactly why you cannot get a job and pay your bills—"

"I have a job!"

"That's not true, Ms. Russo," I tell her condescendingly. "We have all your current information in our file and it shows you have been unemployed for over two years, and honestly I see why—"

"Your information is wrong, Mr. Hart. I'll have you know that I have been an assistant manager at Walmart in Saddle Brook for over two years."

Ding-dong, the bitch is dead!

Confrontational people like Ms. Marie Russo give it up fast. She lost sight of the debt and fought for her honor. And she lost the battle because this is business, but she took it personally. She is told her wages will be levied within 60 days. Her bosses will learn that she is a deadbeat. Her credit will be sabotaged… unless she comes in and pays. If she does that, she will have no damages whatsoever. She has no choice at this point.

For every debtor, there's an angle to play. For every set of circumstances, there's a script. Don't tell me you're not working. I'll tell you where you work. Don't pretend to be your brother Leif. I know exactly what leaf your brother Leif is hiding under. Don't tell me your problems. I'm your number one problem. Forget playing the sympathy card. Show some sympathy for the devil. Don't piss on my back and telling me it's raining or I'll lay your soul to waste. I know where you live, who you live with, who lives next door. I know what you drive, when you drive it, who you sleep with, and who you think about when you sleep with them. I know what's in your dirty underwear. I will scare you into paying me by the sheer extent of my knowledge about you. I'm the boogieman. I'm never going away. Call me Mr. Your Worst Fucking Nightmare. Call me Freddy Krueger the Collector. In fact, call me whatever fucking name you want, but this will never end…*ever*…unless you pay. Do that and I'll disappear from your life forever. *Sweet dreams.*

Don't think for one second you're immune from my tactics. No one is. No one was. Every debtor has a weakness. Let me rephrase: you have a weakness. Maybe it's a job to embarrass you at. A wife. A known boyfriend. An unknown affair. Children. A hidden asset. A secret. There's always something a professional manipulator like me can trick you on, trap you in, or outright blackmail you with. My elite team and I were full-time professionals at discovering that weakness and exploiting it until we got paid.

Furthermore, because I was a crooked Italian American,[39] your only other chance (besides payment) at having your debt forgiven by me was to make me an offer I could not refuse. This is not a discussion I would initiate, but once it was initiated by a female debtor, I was happy to play along.[40] (Sorry, fellas!) There was a whole formula I would apply to these unique scenarios. I had to factor the amount you owed together with your beauty and what sexual favor you were proposing. As you can imagine, it was a very complicated algorithm. First, you needed to be attractive or no deal. You could not just sound attractive. All unattractive women sound attractive on the phone. I learned very quickly that pictures are also not proof of hotness. Every ugly woman in the world has a picture of herself where the shadows, lighting, mood, and coloring are so perfect that they look smoking hot. A picture, therefore, was not admissible proof. You had to physically come to the office and prove your hotness in person for me to consider consummating a deal to forgive your debt.

But really, it was nothing personal when it came to my targets. It was all business—except when it was about pleasure. Like I said, once you paid, you were done with me and my mind-fucking associates forever.[41] I mention it again because I said it repeatedly to my targets—constantly reminding them how they can prevent further harm or suffering. *Confess to me and all the pain goes away. Surrender and be free.* Because it was business, no matter how much you pissed me off, I did not strike again at your weakness, as long as you paid me what you owed. That was part of the bargain. In fact, this was your reward for paying me—dispensation and no hard feelings.

My secretarial staff was easy on the eyes. They were four sexy-and-not-afraid-to-show-it girls who took care of customer relations and daily appointments. They also showed it generously for my male clients and targets whenever it became necessary. *Pussy power!* I mean *girl power!*

Then there were my runners. These guys were on call for me 24/7 and never asked any questions about a job. One runner told me once to not hesitate

---

39 No, you coglione, this is NOT a redundant statement.
40 Frankly, I was surprised by how many debtors offered to "pay through their ass" instead of "pay through the nose."
41 Unless, of course, your dumb ass chooses to not pay another debt.

to call him if I needed him. On his wedding day! Runners were trained experts in surveillance and counter surveillance and were my personal special forces in crime. They cost me a fortune and they were worth every penny. They posed as potential buyers for your house while they downloaded your hard drive. They were utility meter readers who looked through your garbage. They delivered flowers to the wrong addresses. They were your mailmen who undelivered your mail.[42] You see, my runners were there and you never knew it. They were regular customers at Somme's Uniform Store, where uniforms were bought for their diverse positions—everything from a flower delivery guy to FedEx guy to utility company guy to mailman and even a policeman.

Runners competed against each other to be the best so they would get the best gigs. They picked up money, dropped it off, delivered information, spied, filmed, taped, impersonated, intimidated, and whatever else it took to get the job done. When not playing dress-up, they were dressed professionally in suits and drove paid-for Mercedes-Benzes and BMWs. My million-dollar mercenaries.

Right now, I really, really miss my expensive team of information mercenaries. I like to think they're out there, somewhere in the shadows, reading this and missing me just as much. If so, I want you fellas to know I'm more than ready for you to show up one day as my prison guards and walk me outta this bird cage. Just this once. How 'bout it? Come on. You know, for old time's sake...[43]

---

42 In those cases, we would call your phone, cable, or credit card company the next day and ask them to resend the last statement as it "accidentally blew out my window" while driving. This way the subject never knew anything was taken.

43 Hate to give away the ending, but I'm flat busted broke now.

ELEVEN

WHEN EVERYONE AND THEIR MOTHER STARTED GETTING CALLER ID, the collection business went into a collective deep depression. I, however, seized the opportunity. It took me a while to figure it out, but I discovered a way to turn this evolution in technology into my own personal advantage. Of course, the technology needed to support my new idea was way above my expertise, so I did what any criminal entrepreneur in my area did during that time—I summoned Ivan and Alex, the Red computer team from Brooklyn, by way of Moscow. These guys were like having Bill Gates and Steve Jobs devote their brains to wrongdoing.

Before they even sat down, they poured themselves two large glasses of my waiting vodka. This was no ordinary afternoon refresher. Their vodka cocktail was straight up, no ice. There was a filled bucket of inviting ice right next to the warm bottle, but they ignored it. I guess they didn't want to kill the taste. You and I would have puked it up by the second gulp, unless you're Russian. Ivan and Alex drank it down like it was a glass of cold, refreshing water after they had just run a marathon across the Sahara Desert.

With their thirst quenched (for the moment), we sat down and I explained in detail what I wanted developed. They immediately understood what I needed and why and proceeded to confer with each other in Russian for a few minutes. They quoted me fifty grand and said it would take three months to develop. I poured them each another glass and told them I would give them one hundred grand cash and I needed it in two weeks. They moved in to my office the next morning.

As part of the deal, they asked for an unlimited supply of vodka and Red Bull that I found out is referred to as Soviet milk. All day, every day they steadily drank their milk. They were not men; they were machines! They slept separately for only a few hours a day and worked around the clock. One night, I tried drinking their concoction and it launched me into Soviet airspace. I needed to blow American coke to come back down.

Two weeks and two cases of vodka later, my new secret weapon was complete: the Caller ID Jammer. I now had software that allowed me to pre-program the name and telephone number that I wanted to appear on the *receiver's* Caller ID at the time of the call.

My first test was to obtain bank account information for a target named Tom Mayurnik. I nicknamed him Birdman because my client who was after him was a veterinarian, and this asshole had flipped him the proverbial bird when he got the large bill for his sick pit bull. When the vet tried to collect, the Birdman seemingly flew away.

Enter Sandman.

I was not about to hunt and confront a pit bull for money, but I was a wizard at birddogging and hunting down deadbeat, two-legged dogs. The vet had given me a last known address, home phone number, social security number, and the names of his dogs—you can never have enough information. Given that foundation, there were a few ways I could approach my objective. Since I had Birdie's current phone number, I preferred to have him to give me the information himself—always my favorite way to end a goose chase.

First I call the local phone company and save time by accessing their automated billing information center. I key in Tom's phone number and am told last payment amount, the date it posted, and the current amount due. I learn that Tom's last payment was for $212.16 and it posted on March 6th. *My birthday!*

Before I call TomBoy at home, I program my new Caller ID Jammer to read as "Bell Atlantic Collections Dept. 800-339-9911."[44] If you don't pay your phone bill, they shut it off so when Tom sees "Bell Atlantic Collections" on his phone, he picks it up.

"Hello."

In a pleasant, professional tone I state, "May I speak with Mr. Tom Mayurnik, please?"

"This is Tom."

"Mr. Mayurnik, my name is Lou Vafaghool[45] and I am calling from Bell Atlantic Collections Department in regards to your past due amount of $212.16. The reason for my call is that since your account is currently past due, your service is scheduled to be interrupted for non-payment this Friday."

"Why—how, what do you mean? I paid that over a month ago!" You should realize by now that our scam is believed in full by the Birdman.

"Are you sure, Mr. Mayurnik? Because I'm showing a past due amount of $212.16 and as a courtesy we are notifying you prior to interruption—"

"Wait a minute, wait a minute—I paid it!" *Excellent.* Anger is the path to the dark side. And who am I to doubt a Thomas?

"I'm sorry Mr. Mayurnik, but I'm going to need some kind of proof, such as a canceled check."

"I should have my canceled check somewhere in the house."

"Well, if you find that check for me, I may be able to clear this matter up right now on the phone."

TomBoy puts the phone down, and I hear him flipping through his drawers searching for his last bank statement envelope with the canceled checks in them. A few minutes go by and ol' Tom is back on the phone. He has found something that proves me wrong. Everyone loves to be right.

"Hello, yes," he declares. "I have it in my hand."

With Tom comfortable in my web of deceit, it is time to make him feel even more comfortable now. "Is it for $212.16?"

"Yes, that's the exact amount the check was for and it is payable to Bell Atlantic." His tone is very stern because when Tom is right, he's really fucking

44 The number that corresponds with the ID was the valid number for their collection department. All the numbers we programmed in the Caller ID Jammer had to be to a working phone line. This way it would check out and only I (*and now you*) would know the call I'm about to make is a total fraud.
45 Michael Hart needed a break once in a while.

right! *Go TomBoy!*

Now, I already gave Tom the correct amount of the payment, his Caller ID has already told him that I'm from Bell Atlantic, and the check in his hand is the proof he and I are looking for. So what time is it? That's correct! It's time to kill the mockingbird.

"Mr. Mayurnik, if you don't mind, please read me the numbers located on the bottom of the check from left to right so I can check it with the system."

He tweets it to me. I tweet it slowly back to him.

"That's correct," he confirms.

"Okay, Mr. Mayurnik, kindly hold while I verify this. It should only take me a minute." While he's listening to Barry Manilow sing "At the Copa…. Copa-Cabannna!" I am doing a bong hit. Or two. Exhaling, I pick back up the phone. "Mr. Mayurnik?"

"Yes, yes, I'm here."

"Was the check drawn on Fleet Bank?"

"No, no. No! It's First Union Bank, the downtown Camden branch!" He is really chirping now!

"Oh, okay—please hold one more minute. I apologize." Another bong hit and I'm flying high and back on the line. "Mr. Mayurnik, I would like to apologize to you for this inconvenience. For some reason your payment was posted to the wrong account, but I just corrected it and everything is now okay. You will not experience any interruption in service. I posted a $15 credit to your account, which will take about 30 days to process. Again, I apologize for the inconvenience."

It's a wrap! Cut. Print. *That's all folks!* Sylvester ate Tweety Bird. The Coyote finally caught the Road Runner. Bugs fooled Daffy again. Our target deadbeat pheasant has only one more thing to do: watch his money fly away.

I bill my client $500 and they now have Tom's bank account information, the routing number, account number, even his branch location. So yet another birdbrain's account will either be subpoenaed or levied to settle a debt. But at least his phone stayed on and, I assume, his dogs still love him.

✦ ✖ ✦

Using my Caller ID Jammer scam, I made a fortune off baby mamma drama. Here's a typical example: we had been tasked to locate employment information for a target such as our friend Mr. Charles LaSala. Mr. LaSala was far behind on his child-support obligations—which seemingly every baby daddy in New Jersey was—and his ex-wife was trying to file a wage execution. Once a wage execution was in place, the Probation Department would take the money directly from a deadbeat dad's check and pay his ex-wife or baby mamma so she didn't have to deal with that asshole anymore. I had Charles' name, address, and social security number. Although Probation assisted in the execution part of a child support claim, they first needed employment information and were too often not good enough or motivated enough to get it themselves. Enter Daddy Ozzy.

Ring! My Caller ID Jammer is programmed to show Bergen County Judiciary.

"Hello?" answers a male voice cautiously.

"Mr. Charles LaSala, please," and this time I'm using my tough-guy tone.

"This is he."

I look at my watch and see what time it is. Time to show this sperm donor that this daddy means business and has no time for bullshit, even though the whole premise is bullshit. "Is your social security number 145-55-6563?"

"Who's this?" he asks, playing dumb.

"Mr. LaSala, my name is Michael Hart. I'm the chief administrator at the Bergen County Courthouse and this call is being recorded so I am going to ask you again, is your social security number 145-55-6563?"

"Umm…yes, it is," he utters. "How can I help you?"

"Well, Mr. LaSala, you received a subpoena to appear for jury duty the week of May 17th and you did not appear, nor did you reply, which is required by law."

"No sir, I don't recall receiving—"

"Mr. LaSala, the subpoena was sent certified mail and now your failure to comply with it subjects you to prosecution for contempt of court. And I promise you that you won't be the first person to lose your case claiming you didn't receive the subpoena."

Pause. I want to do a bong hit, but I have to stay with this dipshit to drop some bait. "Now, Mr. LaSala, I can exempt you in our system under Article 6-42 for medical reasons or Article 6-43B if you are working and your employer does not pay your wages for jury duty." *Pause.* "Mr. LaSala, are you on any kind of disability?"

"No."

"Where do you work?"

"Shop Rite in Garfield," he admits. "I'm the deli manager."

"Well, then you most likely meet the 6-43B exemption. Give me the phone number to your department and my secretary will confirm your exemption."

I get the number and hang up. Five minutes, 500 bucks. *The grand Daddy always delivers!*

TWELVE

BANK ROBBERY JUST DOESN'T PAY ANYMORE. IT HAD A GOOD RUN THOUGH. For almost 500 years, any petty thief could walk into any standing bank disguised, armed with a real or fake weapon, and—if they're quick, calculated, and lucky—leave less than three minutes later hoping to be 20 grand richer in today's dollars. Any longer of a timeframe or an attempt to steal any more money than that virtually guarantees bad results. Even in that pressurized, two-minute window, there is a good chance someone ruins your day by slipping you a dye pack or triggering the silent alarm. If they do either, or if you fail to get away unidentifiable and expeditiously, you'll face 20 years in prison. Twenty fucking years in a human vault for a measly 20 grand? The math doesn't add up in my book. Too much risk for only a weekend's worth of cocaine.

So I had to figure out a better way...

Although DRL offered information of all kinds, the hidden treasure was in the most difficult to unearth information there is—banking. Access to banking information, I realized, could be merchandised for more money than all the others combined. It was the most valuable commodity in the industry. And it was the most elusive.

No one else was offering bank account information as a specialty because, quite frankly, they were not crazy, corrupt, or shrewd enough to go after it. To figure out a way to get inside and uncover banking secrets, I first had to prepare patiently, which was not one of my virtues. Famous crimes aren't made overnight, folks. I had to absorb all I possibly could about how the banking profession operated. Like any burglar, I cased my target. But I did it for years. And my casing was different, as I was not planning to stick them up for their money. Too primitive. Too limited. Too loud. Too risky.

Instead, I was plotting to rob their information, over and over again, nicely and quietly, and then sell it. In order to accomplish this, I could not simply slip a politely worded ransom note at the counter. I needed to type my demands literally into their computers and have it spit out pay dirt. Oh yeah, and without anyone suspecting anything at all. *Wish me luck!*

If my life has taught me anything (and if this story has taught you anything), it's that everyone and everything is vulnerable somehow, somewhere, some place, some time. After years of analyzing banks, I finally concluded the primary vulnerability for the banking industry was twofold:

1. Their false sense of internal security

2. Liberal employee access

For security purposes, banks have always been focused on external threats, such as robberies, and rightfully so, since they have been robbed since their birth. They are also required, by market forces and sometimes force of law, to operate in high crime areas. This further focuses their security attention to physical defense against outside threats that walk into their branches. To an increasing extent in the late 90s, banks were focusing on thwarting computer hacks. Y2K kept them up at night worried for over a year. Online banking was years off, but software viruses were not. Again, these were still external threats in nature. The dipshits in charge of securing the banking industry worried about people they didn't know, but not about those they did know. You are always most vulnerable in life where you feel most comfortable. That's why only people you trust can betray you.

That is not to say internal threats were not safeguarded against. The banking profession required clean records. Human resources conducted extensive background checks. The adverse event reporting process was strictly governed. Cameras were everywhere. Multiple employees were required for many types of transactions. Approvals and authorizations were necessary on other transactions. Training was constant. Testing was routine. Evaluations were regular. Proper dress was required. You needed to prove your work. Count in, then count out your drawer. Call in when you were opening the door. Call out when you closed it for the night. Enter your code to access rooms. And so on. All the aforementioned Big Brother measures were strategically in place to give employees, managers, and even officers an omnipresent sense of the fact that they would have zero fucking chance of stealing successfully.

But no high-paid boardroom executive in an Armani suit or security officer in the world of banking ever stopped and realized what someone with a high school diploma eventually determined—that banks paid shitty entry-level wages and typically gave those same employees access to their entire universe of data so they could best serve their customers. To top it off, those employees by and large had zero loyalty to their employers and were not inclined to like their supervisors either. Put it all together in a felonious fishbowl and a shark like me saw vulnerability (read: *profitability*) in the waters. And it was time to start the process of fishing.

With the weakness identified, my attack needed to be planned with the details of a military invasion. My initial target was the banking industry's Achilles heel—their tellers. Conceivably, if I was unable to convert tellers to the dark side, I could alternatively plant converted ones into those positions. Conversion of existing tellers was the first phase I attempted. My years in collections had filled my Rolodex with several high-level bank employees who I traded favors or bribes with in the past, but there were a lot of fucking banks and not enough corrupt and disloyal managers or executives.

With tellers in my riflescope, my weapon to convert them was not money— at least not initially. It was charm. Charm builds trust. Money actually makes people nervous at first. Once trust was established, a confidential financial relationship—we are talking about having people commit felonies here—could be broached. If the trust built is strong enough, then money becomes an easily introduced incentive. This is the formula in which all great criminal empires were built upon. However, I assure you none of them employed the power of the penis as much as mine.

Now, I am well aware of the gender differences you have to be cognizant of in dealing with men and women for illegitimate business purposes. I read that book *Women Are From Mars and Men Have A Penus*. Although charm works well on both men and women, it certainly works better on women if you're a man. And vice versa. Fortunately, low-level bank tellers were predominately female. My entire criminal enterprise would end up primarily dependent upon young girls making $8.50 an hour.

With targeting complete, I approached them first as a customer interested in opening an account—new to the area, young, single, definitely well-off financially, full of humor, smiles, and wit (*and shit*). Within two weeks, I'd opened dozens of accounts at different banks that I wanted to rob. This allowed me the opportunity to spend time in branches, witness their operations, and see their corporate culture up close. I scouted tellers, plus all the douchebag managers. I watched interoffice relations and got a sense of their job morale. *Were they happy? Were they struggling financially? Single mothers? Students? Did they like their manager? And most importantly, were they attracted to me or my money?*

Over the coming weeks, I became a regular customer. Always smiling, upbeat, making sizable deposits, withdrawals and, most importantly, complimenting the women. My positive energy and free spirit brought in a breath of fresh air. Most bank customers are like you—exhausting and boring. My lifestyle was fast and fun. I was young and successful, always with a glow on my face and pep to my step. Before long, I was generally able to zero-in on the head teller, or better stated, have her zero-in on servicing my transactions whenever I stepped through the doors. Before long, I had established a pseudo-dating, or friends-with-benefits, kind of relationship at several major banks in the area. None of this could appear rushed or fake. Boy, was that exhausting work. And expensive.

I know what you're wondering so let's get it out of the way so we never have to address it again. The answer to your question is—of course not! This was business, yes, mixed together with monkey business, but business nevertheless. I didn't have the time or the patience to court the hottest teller at every bank. Some were drop dead gorgeous, but that was because they happened to put out the proper signals to me. Others were, let's just say, not the hottest. Now let's carry on, shall we?

Against my true nature and depravity, my strategy was not to use sex to recruit my soldiers. If I based the trust on sex, I don't think it would have worked for very long. Therefore, and unfortunately for them, I had to get into their hearts before their panties.

With trust being the objective, I could not make the first move physically. Psychologically, I made the first five moves but physically, the first move had to be theirs, not mine. It was a challenge to keep track of all the schooling, family issues, work issues, kids, and other bullshit I had to pretend like I cared about, but patience and listening pays off. *Men, there's a lesson in there somewhere, even if you don't aspire to rob banks—listen more and don't lead with your wanker when it comes to women. And good luck with that!*

Discreetly, without making it a point, I invited them into Ozzy's world of show-and-tell. I was mysterious and they were curious. The new sports car. The view from the pimped-out condo. And, of course, the shoes. Women love shoes! Not just their shoes. I learned my footwear was equally important to women so I bought dozens of pairs.

When they asked, I told them, "I'm in the collection business." Being young, highly successful, last-named Lembo, and full of cash forced them to do the math about "the collection business." However, I did not want to be viewed as illegitimate and especially not mobbed-up. That would scare most people away, even with trust. I went through extensive lengths to explain the how I was in the legitimate side of the industry. This presentation[46] was also my opportunity to educate them about how rewarding and easy information brokering can be for someone like them. By that time, it appeared to them like I only opened up about my work and thought about their participation in it because of the wonderful trust and special bond I felt with them. Not that I had been conspiring to recruit them since before our first hello…

Inevitably, they would tell me about how they were in debt or got a call or dreaded letter from a collection agency. This was my opportunity to provide them with comfort and answer all of their credit questions. From credit scores to auto loans to student loans, I knew it all and was now their trusted credit and financial adviser. Later on, clearing up their financial and credit problems became quid pro quo for the crimes they were abetting me on.

---

46 This was always done outside of the bank and usually in a swank restaurant where the lighting was sexy and the menu exotic.

Inside the banks, cameras are always pointed at the customers or the money, not so much at the employees. The fake cop—I mean, security guard—is always by the door, not by the tellers. His job is to watch the customers. What he didn't watch were the employees, except when he was hitting on the cutest ones, which was constantly.[47]

Tellers work systematically. Independent thinking is not permitted. Discretion is not allowed. Procedures dominate a banker's day. Fail to comply and you are written up on the spot. No exceptions allowed. A banker's mannerisms and language in person and on the phone are scripted by their bosses. They pull money from the middle drawer, never the top drawer. Why? Because the top ones are hooked up to the alarm system. When they had to go into the vault or open the ATM, they had to do it as a pair, like when girls go to the bathroom. In the banking world it is called *dual control*. Everywhere else it is called *dual pee-pee*.

Checks were another layer of the security processes I studied. Every time you touch one, there are oils that capture your fingerprints. Checks also have watermarks in them to verify if they are real. I got acquainted with all the secrets of *funny money* and about all the different kinds of paper used. From the way that it feels to the way it folds, crumples, and burns. I studied it all with the help of my insiders who were happy to educate me after hours at a nice restaurant or in bed.

If there was a robber inside, bank employees were trained to never hit the silent alarm. Why? Because doing so would likely lead to a hostage situation. They had to wait until the perpetrator is on his way out. Once he is leaving, he ain't coming back to say *I told you not to do that.* Speaking of alarms, where are the buttons? Where do they ring? I learned it all. I also learned about dye-packs, armored trucks, and where the money went after it leaves the building. All that learned, I was still not planning to rob their money by force one day. I was planning to steal their information daily by finesse.

I memorized every bank routing number, how many digits in total made up each bank account number, what digits all the different type of accounts started with, how a wire was processed, certified funds approved, and the most important question of all—what data and information was accessible to an employee about a customer. That data and information was the ultimate target.

    My inside girls explained to me in bed what types of identification were

47 Note to security guards: Women like men in real uniforms, not fake ones.

required to open an account. They also walked me through why, before the account is opened, they had to excuse themselves and go to the back office. Turns out they were required to contact Chex-Systems, a credit reporting system for banks. The purpose of that call is to check out the prospect. The teller provides the bank's secret code and learns if the potential customer in the chair has been naughty or nice to other banks. Moreover, they tell you what other banks have recently inquired about your applicant. Of course, these secret codes were also whispered into my ear and later entered into my computer.

It was exhausting and expensive, but the seeds I sowed (along with my wild oats) with my teller girls would pay off for many years. Little did they know—hell, little did I know—how far I would end up taking my quest to steal the most precious and protected data from banks.

THIRTEEN

THANK YOU FOR CALLING FIRST UNION BANK, HOW MAY I HELP YOU?"
I hang up; I didn't like *his* voice. I spent years perfecting the schmooze
of ladies at banks, not men.

I dial the same number again. This time the voice sounds ideal. "Thank you
for calling First Union Bank, this is Julie. How may I assist you today?"[48]

Now she is definitely young, which doesn't necessarily mean, but
nevertheless rhymes with dumb. Just sayin'. As usual, I imagine her with perky
breasts encased in a very tight sweater. I also visualize that underneath her
white skirt is a thong panty, either a light blue or maybe pink with a little white
bow in front barely covering her shaved slice. Either color will do, really. I then
put together a whole scene in my mind about how she is telling me she just
learned her fiancé was cheating on her with her best friend while we are alone

---

48 Now I could have called any branch, but I called the southernmost First Union
Bank located in New Jersey. Why? Because northern New Jersey has more assholes
per capita than southern New Jersey.

inside the bank vault at night.[49]

"Hi Julie, this is Michael Hart from Fleet Bank.[50] How are you today?"

"Fine, thank you. And you?"

"Oh, I'll be a lot better if you can solve my predicament." *Right away I'm appealing to her professional courtesy.*

"I'll try." *Great. Time to get down to business.*

My target is Jake Moore who skipped out on his apartment lease. My client is the attorney for Golden Rentals, Jake's former landlord. The attorney sends the account to me because he needs information in order to complete collections. The file contains a civil court judgment against Jake for $13,672 with all the fees and interest and is docketed in Bergen County. It also has an address that was used to serve the summons, social security number, date of birth, and rental application with First Union Bank listed as a bank reference, but no account number and no working phone number.

Looks like Jake the Snake is playing *catch me if you can*. I can. Time for Jake's enema. That's why the Caller ID reads "Fleet Bank" on her desk phone.

"Julie, I'm trying to send a wire to a customer of yours. His name is Jake Moore. I have your routing number. And unfortunately, besides the first digit of four on his account, my coffee spill ruined the slip!"[51]

"Oh, no!" my girl Julie declares. *Peer sympathy. Just what I was looking for.*

"I know, I know. I'm so embarrassed. I was rushing to go to lunch and made a mess. Is there anything else I can provide you with to get this done so you can spare me the embarrassment of having to contact the customer again and being written up?" *Bankers can relate to these exact predicaments.*

"Well, do you have a social? I may be able to cross reference using that."

"Yes, oh gosh, thank you so much. It's 159-60-5770."

"There it is," she replies. *Bingo!*

"You show a Mr. Jake Moore?" I ask.

"Yes, I do. Let me give you the correct account number."

---

49 You may ask where I am going with this and why any of it matters to the story. Well, it matters nothing to the story...but everything to my jailhouse imagination right now.

50 Yes, there is actually a bank named after an enema brand.

51 How do I have the routing number? My computer files have all the bank routing numbers. I also know their checking account numbers start with the number four and are eleven digits in length.

"God bless you. You really are my savior."[52] She reads it off to me. *I'm not done though.* "Thank you so much, Julie! Now the account is still open; correct?"

"Yes, it is."

"And I could get that wire in before 3pm?"

"You should not have a problem; you have a whole hour."

"Great, Julie. I thank you so much."

"My pleasure, Michael. Have a nice day."

After I hang up, I enter Julie's information into my computer system, with the note "perky and helpful" for future reference. Then, armed with soon-to-be-broke Mr. Moore's information, I dial the First Union 1-800 customer service number, which is handled out of South Carolina. *Even nicer!*

"Thank you for calling First Union customer service. This is Michelle. How may I help you?" *Well, well, Michelle, oh my darling Southern belle.* This girl sounds so nice that I almost feel guilty about lying. *Almost.*

"Hi Michelle, my name is Jake Moore. I'm doing my monthly bills and I need to check my current balance."

"Sure, Jake. No problem. What is your account number?" I read it to her slowly and then "my" social security number and address without being asked as if I have done this drill before. Act like you've been there before and you can go anywhere in life. Including prison.

"Okay now, Jake—I have your information here. Your current balance is $8,220.19."

"Thank you. Have a blessed day!"??

So now I have my target's account number and current balance, but it's not enough to cover what he owes so I need to crawl even further up Jake's ass and identify his wages to garnish. Without a working number or physically staking him out (too costly), it is difficult to discover a place of employment. Unless you are me.

Let's review. We have Jake's name, address, bank account number, and social security number. But we don't know where he works. *Hmmmm....who does?* The State of New Jersey Department of Labor, that's who! These are the folks you pay state taxes to if you work in the Garden State.[53]

---

52 I typically invoked the Lord to disguise the devil.
53 Incidentally, I always found *Garden State* to be a very misleading nickname for a state that smells mainly of industrial horseshit.

A quick programming of my Caller ID Jammer to read "Jake Moore" with the direct number back to my desk and it's time to dial the number for the Labor Department.

"Unemployment Department." A man's voice and not friendly-sounding, but I am trapped with this one. State workers are assholes in general, male ones in particular, but we should be okay on this one because I don't need any sympathy. If you're a state worker, sorry to break the news to you but everyone who interacts with you thinks you're an asshole. I know what you're thinking and the answer is—*No! You definitely are not an exception to that rule.* Anyway, back to the fraud at hand.

"Yes, I hope you can help me," I say. "I was working through a temp service and was hired midway as a full-time seasonal employee. I'm about to apply for unemployment benefits and don't know who to list as my actual employer."

"What is your social security number?"

I give it to him and add my name and address.

"I show that your wages are being paid through Toys-R-Us; is that correct?"

"Yes, but the problem is I got the job through Accu-temps in Newark."

"Well, when filing, you need to list Toys-R-Us because that is your base employer who is paying the payroll taxes."

"What address should I use?"

"It looks like the payroll is handled out of the headquarters in Rochelle Park, New Jersey. The physical address is 2100 Passaic Avenue, ZIP 07609."

"Okay. I will do that." *Man, he was pretty helpful for an asshole.*

We now have employment information to go with his bank information. But I do not know if he still works at Toys-R-Us and if so, what exact store he works in.

Luckily, I have a scam solution for every problem. Remember, I'm not being paid by my time so I have no time to waste.[54] And time separates good collectors from great ones. Good ones, at this point, would spend an hour calling Toys-R-Us stores starting with the closest to his last known address. I zero in on the payroll department at corporate headquarters because it offers the fastest kill.

"Thank you for calling Toys-R-Us. How may I direct your call?"

"Personnel or payroll, whichever is free to take my call." Both have the information I need and I don't have time to stay on hold like you do.

54 Now I have plenty of time to waste.

"Personnel. Can I help you?"

"Yes—this is Michael Hart with Federal Express dispatch in Maywood, New Jersey." Caller ID programmed accordingly, just in case you were wondering.

"How can I help you?"

"I have a driver who went out to your location at 2100 Passaic Avenue over in Rochelle Park trying to deliver a package to an employee by the name of Jake Moore. The driver was told he does not work at that location. Can you do me and him a favor and look him up? This package is from the State of New Jersey Division of Taxation in Trenton, New Jersey, so I want to make sure it gets to him."

He falls for the fake gravity of the situation. No one wants to stand in the way of the taxman. "He's at our Route 23 location in Wayne."

"Thank you. I will re-route the package and he should have it later on today."

I dial the Wayne store directly and ask, "Hey, is Jake working today?" It is good to use only first names or nicknames when you are lying about someone at their workplace, like you know them well.

"Yes, he is. He'll be in at three." *Bingo! Confirmation, bitches!*

I write up both a wage execution and bank levy and send the information to my attorney client who immediately begins the process of legally fist-fucking our boy Jake right through the pants. First, he files what is called a writ of execution with the court where the civil judgment is docketed. The court then hands it over to an appointed constable who adds his fee and delivers a notice of levy to the nearest First Union. Jake's bank account gets frozen right then and there. The court then drains it and pays my client. To secure the balance, the constable sends a notice of wage execution to Toys-R-Us, which states they must comply with a court order and garnish Mr. (please no) Moore's paycheck weekly until the judgment amount is paid with interest running. So basically now the court is doing all the work, acting as my client's own personal collection agency. Jake won't know what hit him.

And he'll never find out how it was all done.

And he'll never know I was involved.

I bill my attorney client $500 for the information. It cost me nothing but 30 minutes of my time. The attorney pays me the $500 and then adds it to the cost of the judgment as an expense so really it cost him nothing to hire me to do his dirty work.

✦ ◼ ✦

My masterful pretext team and I scammed the phone companies, cable, social security, water, tax assessors, and courts for information all day. And then we partied all night. Soon, we started to party all day while working. The numbers we were generating seemed like riches but they were peanuts compared to what was about to come.

So was the partying.

So was the risk.

FOURTEEN

B EFORE LONG, I SCORED A CHEX-SYSTEMS GIRL CONNECTION.
"Thank you for calling Chex-Systems. What is your name and
authorization code?"

"Hi, this is Jen at Natwest Bank. My code is 345122." It's really Barbara
from my office. Women are genetically superior pretexters, as they are not
expected to be lowlife scammers like men. For all my male and lesbian readers,
Barbara is long-legged, with straight dark hair, dark eyes, and light skin. More
importantly, her most pronounced feature, by far, was her tremendous balloon
lips. They were so big and puffy that the rest of my staff referred to her as Daffy
Duck behind her back. I found their nickname to be sexist, rude, and offensive.
So I made everyone change it to Daisy Duck. Because Barbara worked for me,
she used those fat lips for lying and…anyway, back to the call—

"Okay, Jen. Go ahead please."

"Thank you. I need to clear five applicants for the branch please." As
mentioned, Chex-Systems is the independent company that housed data on all

bad accounts for the banking industry.[55] They also kept records on all inquiries pertaining to a subject. One by one, orgasm by orgasm, I acquired the code for each bank from my little insiders. Some whispered it in my ear. Others screamed it out during sex. In any event, I had them all so it was time to put them to immoral use.

"Please give them to me one at a time," our Chex girl requests.

Before she does, Barbara first quacks—I mean, instructs, "I need you to tell me if they're in your system and if there have been any inquires on them within the last 180 days."

"No problem. Proceed."

Barbara provides all the targets' names and social security numbers and we learn[56] whether they are currently in Chex-Systems or not, which we really don't care about. What we do care about is the last inquiry on the bank. That tells us if, when, and where a target tried to or did open a bank account.

Remember I told you prior to opening up any bank account the customer service rep always walked into the back to call Chex-Systems first. Although we are not positive if the account was opened that day, we do know which banks our targets tried to open an account at. We go down the list of banks using the wire pretext I used with Mr. Moore to find accounts. Each account we find is billed out $500. A real bargain for the necessary information a creditor needs in order to collect thousands of dollars from a hidden debtor in less time than it takes to finish a bowl of cereal.

The vast majority of the debtors we were hired to dig up were the scumbags of society. *I know—it takes a scumbag to know one.* Our targets had every opportunity to make payment arrangements in order to settle debts or even file for bankruptcy before the claim reached my office, and they refused to. They were hiding from their responsibilities and hiding from the law by ignoring bills, collection letters, civil court summonses, etc. But they could not ignore Ozzy once their account landed at DRL.

I am not disparaging my targets to make myself look better. I was a villain. We all agree on that. We can also agree that Michael Hart was a singular scum-sucking debtor and he was me. I'm just stating the facts about debtors. They (including me) were not deadbeats who missed one or two payments on their

---

55 They also make a nice variety of cereals.

56 Which is "earn" with an "L" added to it.

credit cards. Some (not me) were truly sympathetic figures that were dealt an unfortunate set of circumstances and came upon hard times. Whenever I encountered these legitimate sympathy cases, I still had to press on and go for their jugular. I truly did not want to at times, but still I had to. If not, my percentages would go down and I would lose my clients. Unfortunately, sometimes you catch a few dolphins when you're fishing for sharks. However, by and large, the debtors I targeted were pathetic assholes or professional scam artists (or both), no different than I was, except in vision and results. Did my targets' dubious morality somehow make me feel better about my deceitful tactics? Shit yeah, it did!

What pissed me off most after my arrest was that the media never reported my story in its entirety. I know—*Whah! Whah! Whah!* I'm not crying about it and the headlines were certainly true that I masterminded all that money to change hands, but it was also true, and largely undisclosed by reporters, that I assisted in collecting millions upon millions of dollars in debt such as child support arrears. The law couldn't deliver justice like that. The law will never be able to deliver justice like that. The law is not smart enough. The law is not fast enough. The law and the people who enforce it are definitely not motivated enough. Don't believe me? Spend a day in family court. Just one day—and I promise you will see how unjust the legal system is. Who was the best at attaining justice for countless neglected children? Ozzy was. That's who.

Sallie Mae is the term used for the student loan division of the federal government. Any student in need of assistance for their education calls her. For some reason, just the name Sallie Mae always turned me on. I always pictured Sallie Mae as a nymphomaniac virgin country girl with cute little pigtails and Daisy Dukes that desperately needed a young stud just like me—*hey, it's my fantasy*—to gallop in and seize her virginity over a stack of hay bales.[57]

My chance to fulfill my Sallie Mae I-bang-you fantasy came the day I met with a 20-year-old foreign exchange student from France.[58] A female friend of mine sent her over to me because I was in the credit business and "may be able to help her fill out her student aid forms."

---

57 Again, this fantasy has nothing to do with the story but everything to do with confinement.
58 I know this already sounds like a perfect plot for porn and truthfully, that's why it made the cut for this book.

Her name was Gwen, not that it mattered. Actually, truth be told, I forgot her name. There have been a lot of miles of coke traveled since then. What really mattered is she was smoking Euro-hot, which means hot with a foreign accent.

When she arrived, I was crazy busy and would have otherwise passed her off to one of my workers until I saw her and Little Ozzy immediately yelled from inside my pants "Don't let me down! Please!" So, of course, I immediately explained to her how complicated her matter was (without knowing anything at all about it) and scheduled an appointment with her at my condo that evening so I could give her the undivided attention that her critical matter required.

She came into my condo wearing a short black leather skirt that evening. To welcome her properly on behalf of all American men, I was chilling a bottle of Perrier-Jouët Rosé, one of the finest from her homeland. Turns out, she was not only Euro-hot, she was Euro-thirsty for champagne. I couldn't wait to show her I had a Euro-cut penis. I quickly realized she wasn't drinking at her host family's house so she was attempting to make up for the dry mouth she developed over the past few months.

After an hour of drinking, laughing over mimicking each other's accents, and reviewing her loan paperwork, Gwen began rubbing my leg under the table. I was most offended so I slid my hand up her skirt to show her how it feels. She was not offended. In fact, she opened her legs wide and put her head all the way back. When my hand arrived at its destination (there was no panty armor), it was so warm and wet that it felt like I was feeding a horse. Apparently, America had been neglecting this French firecracker for a while. *It was time we all started treating our immigrants better!*

I'm not one to brag, but my ability to reload my pistol is what separates me from the rest of my gender. Little Ozzy's sexual recuperative powers are, and will always be, the key to my prowess. Most men are useless after they flatten out, but I was able to inflate my love balloon again within minutes. To a certain extent, I was born with a genetically gifted groin, but I developed it into super penis status through a perfect cocktail of cocaine, Viagra, and ecstasy. That is my secret formula for marathon sex and now you have the recipe. All you need to do is be willing to commit a couple of crimes to get the right ingredients. I committed well over 10,000 drug offenses before I was 40 years old. I mention that solely to inspire you to follow your wet dreams and never let anyone say you can't do something (or someone).

Once you gather the goods, don't go mixing them all together in a blender with your favorite berries for a smoothie. Timing is critical in life and even more so in the life of a sexual misfit. Viagra always needs to be taken first, approximately 30 minutes from cranking up. Ecstasy should then go down about fifteen minutes out. Then, just before blast off, coke is the final turbo injection for your engine. Careful though. Only a little coke. Too much backfires. In fact, cocaine can be your sexual spinach or kryptonite. I learned that the hard way. And the soft way.

If you have never tried this formula, find your partner(s) now and follow the above instructions. I'll wait right here until you're done…

…How was it? Strong like a bull, eh? Did you feel like you could have rammed your penis through a slab of concrete? I call that sidewalk sex. Boy, do I miss those times. In prison, we can only have mattress sex. Anyway, I told you if you follow my filthy fucking advice, you will achieve your highest sexual plateaus. I may have robbed your information in the past, but don't say I'm not looking out for you now. Or at least your loins. You're welcome.

My turbo cocktail worked wonders that night. Gwen even told me that I was a better lover than French men, which I think statistics prove is a really big compliment. I also learned if a foreign woman is talking to me in a language I don't understand, I cum much faster and further. Gwen could have been screaming in French "I can't feel your dick 'cause it's so tiny," but it came through to my ears as "I love your rhinoceros cock." Either way, I had an all-access pass to all her rides that glorious evening.

After our international fuck fest, we got back to the paperwork. Gwen suddenly confessed that she hated this country—even after several orgasms—and did not want to go to school here anymore. The dark light bulb in my head immediately turned on. It never turns off, really. In the end, Gwen ended up going back home and conveniently forgot to take the two $25,000 checks she was sent from Sallie Mae to my house long after she was back in France. Although they were both payable to Gwen Goulet, I had a bank contact work it out so that I was able to deposit the checks into my account by showing Gwen "on paper" was living with me. I sent Gwen 2,000 bucks, which she thought was a 50/50 split.[59]

---

59 Don't judge me. She was the one who abandoned me after a one-night stand.

The government will be happy to know that I used the money to continue my own education in the form of a brand new Corvette. I named her Sallie Mae after the girl who I fucked silly for it. *Merci, Sallie! And merci, Gwen! Or whatever your name is. I will never forget our ménage à trois!*

But my favorite pretext of all time was not conducted for profit. It was for pure pleasure at the direct expense of Mamma Lembo.

Mamma Lembo and I always had a great relationship, especially early on, before my vices, greed, and criminality consumed me completely. Even after I became a total degenerate, I was still her baby boy degenerate, so she visited my office on a weekly basis with lunch for the crew. She also got to pick up a little shopping money courtesy of her son's pretext palace.

Well, one day she is serving lunch and hears everyone on the phone hammering away at targets with our arsenal of lies. She hears people handing over their personal information left and right. Finally, I guess she just couldn't take it anymore. When we sat down to start feasting on her fine pasta, she tells us how stupid the people we dealt with were and how she would "never, ever-a fall-a for-a something like-a 'dis."

I, of course, pretended not to hear her comment and uttered, "Pass the cheese, please."

As soon as Mamma Lembo walked out the door, I told Barbara to set a ticker on my calendar for two weeks from today and label it "Operation Mamma." Two weeks passed and I told everyone to come into my office and I hit the speakerphone button:

"Elloo," I knew Mamma's schedule so I call her just when she finishes watching television and starts to get ready for bed. When she looked at her Caller ID, it read "Bergen County Police."

"May I please speak to a Mr. or Mrs. Lembo?" My voice is so well disguised it would fool my own mother, which was exactly what I was doing.

"Dis is-a Mrs. Lembo."

"Mrs. Lembo, this is Sergeant Slaughter from the Bergen County Police. I'm sorry I am contacting you this evening, but we arrested your son, Orazio Jr., for drinking, smoking pot, and lewd behavior in public." *Houston, we have deceit! Well, at least as far as the arrest part goes.*

"Waaat-ah!"

"Yes, Mrs. Lembo, your son was a mess." This was actually true.

"He-a smoking a-pot! Again! And he-a drink! That son-of-ma bitch!" I did those things every night.

"Yes, Mrs. Lembo, he certainly is, plus he is also being charged with lewd behavior in public." That was true only on most nights.

"What's-a dis lewdie?" she asks. I think "lewdie" translated means someone who is lewd often. Or maybe it is not even a word. Anyway—

"Well, Mrs. Lembo, we found him outside the bar smoking marijuana and waving his pee-pee around to everyone who was walking by. And it was only happy hour!"

"He-a WHAT! No-oh-a my God!" My mother is now telling my father in Italian that I was high, drunk, and flashing my *pene* (do I need to translate that to Italian?) to a bunch of *innocent* people outside a bar. I guess if they were *guilty* people, she thinks it would not be so obscene to snake them.

My father starts yelling back at her "Disonore! Disonore!" which means *disgrace* in Italian. I cut back in—

"Mrs. Lembo, unless he makes bail within the next 30 minutes, I'm afraid we're going to have to take him down to the county jail for the night."

"In-a jail? No-a, no-a please!"

"Can you pay the bail for him? It's $1,000."

"One-a thousand dollars! Oh-that-a son-a ma-bitch!" I could have told her $29.99 and she would have bugged out the same way. "You take-a credit card?"

"Yes, of course we do." Which, of course, they don't, if this was real.

"Let-a me get-a my-a purse." Now, my parents are both screaming back and forth at each other over whose fault it is that I grew up this way. They start yelling about how my brother Joe would never do something like that. All of the sudden, my mother switches to the cordless phone so she could be mobile. She always complained how she could never hear well on the cordless. So I used it to my advantage.

"I-a got-a da card here."

"Okay, Mrs. Lembo. Can you read me the card number?"

"It's-a 5-a-1-a-2-a-1-a," she begins.

"Louder, Mrs. Lembo, please, I can't hear you."

"5-a-1-a-2-a-1-a," she says louder. By the way, her normal tone is way louder than normal people.

"You'll have to speak louder, Mrs. Lembo!"

"5-a-1-a-2-a-1-a-6-a-1-a-8-a-4-a-7-a-3-a-8-a-7-a-2-a-2-a-1-a-3-a!"

She just woke up the people next door.

"Okay, thank you. I got it. What is the expiration date?"

"It's-a October-a 96-a."

"Are you sure?"

"Yes-a! October-a 1996!" Marty is sitting next to me laughing his ass off, but covering his mouth with the rest of my office. He whispers for me to say something about my mother's head because she has such a big head for a little body. She was built like a bobble head Italian lady.

"Now Mrs. Lembo, how big is this card?"

"What-a you mean how-a big?"

"The card—Mrs. Lembo is it standard size, or is it jumbo, like your head?"

"What-a you said?"

"Your head is jumbo. Is the card jumbo also?"

"No-a it's a Master-a-Card!" Everyone is now on the floor of my office laughing uncontrollably.

"Oh, I see. And what color is this MasterCard?"

"Da color?"

"Yes, the color?"

"It's-a navy blue."

"Navy blue. Okay then. Now Mrs. Lembo, hold the card and shake it real fast, and tell me if it turns red."

"What-a you-a mean-a by shake-a da card?"

"Shake it, Mrs. Lembo! Shake it!"

"I-a shake-a, I-a shake-a!"

"Did it turn red?"

"No-a no-a. It's-a still-a navy blue." Pee is running down the legs of some of my employees.

"Okay, Mrs. Lembo, now, before I process the charge, would you like to add a tip?"

"A tip-a! For-a what?"

"The PBA Association. If you donate, we will send you a nice decal that you can put in your car window."

"No-a! I no-a give you-a tip-a! You-a crazy!"

"Fine, Mrs. Lembo, be like that. When you hear the sound of the beep, say 'no tip.' Ready?"

I press the 5 button. *Beep!*

"No-a tip."

"Sorry, Mrs. Lembo, it did not register. Try it again."

I press the 5 button again. *Beep!*

"No-a tip!" she shouts.

"Louder, Mrs. Lembo. Please, you must speak louder."

Beep!

"No-a tip! No-a tip!" I know that my father is looking at her like she fucking crazy.

"One more time, but louder and faster, Mrs. Lembo!"

Beep!

"NO-A TIP! NO-A TIP! NO-A TIP! NO-A TIP!" My mother is now screaming so loud we could hear her even if we weren't on the phone with her. I know how my mother gets when she is all excited—I can actually see all kinds of spit flying out of her mouth right through the phone.

"Now, Mrs. Lembo, are you tired yet?"

"What-a you-a mean, am I-a tired yet?"

"Are you tired?" She tells me father in Italian that I want to know if she is tired. My father tells her to ask me why I want to know.

"Why-a you-a want-a to know?"

"It's just a question. You sound tired, that's all."

"I'm-a gonna kill-a my-a son-a when I-a see him, and you-a gonna take-a me-a to jail-a!"

"Mrs. Lembo please, calm down. That's your son!"

"My-a son-a! He-a drink!! He-a smoke-a pot!! He-a drive-a me-a crazy all-a my life!"

"Okay Mrs. Lembo, do you have a pen?"

"Let-a me-a get-a one."

She gets the pen and is ready to write. I tell her this, "Please write this down; this is your confirmation number. Are you ready?"

"Yes-a. I-a ready." She is still breathing heavy from all the yelling.

"Okay. It's VA---FA---GOOL!"[60] and I hung up.

---

60 This means *fuck you* in Italian.

Once my mother heard that, she knew what time it was. The next day I got a call from my father, who was still laughing. He told me my mother was also laughing all night.

Her son was a degenerate, but he could make anyone and their mother act like a fool.

My old man and his two 'lil monkeys. The youngest monkey is unfortunately locked in a cage right now.

Teenage Wasteland

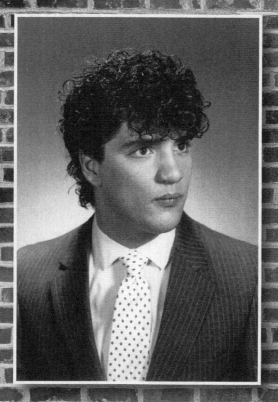

In high school, I worked for wiseguys so no one made fun of my perm-mullet.

Me and Joe. Physically is where the similarities ended.

The King and I

One of my Bergen County Jailbreak celebrations. Her name was Bella. Just like all the other girls I partied with.

Driving my train, high on cocaine.

Master of disguises
and ceremonies.
For more than ten
years, I routinely
spent a couple
grand partying
every night.

The last picture I will ever take
with my family.

FIFTEEN

T O BE CONSIDERED A TRUE INFORMATION BROKERAGE SERVICE, I needed to have the proper staff. Runners were underground and not the kind of staff we included on our letterhead. I found the face of DRL in Uncle Sam, a former Marine who served as military police for over 20 years. He became my staff PI and gave us an air of legitimacy.

Uncle Sam was a perfect face for DRL, and he possessed the proper PI credential that I could promote publicly. Uncle Sam's license also gave me another license to steal. Licensed PIs have access to information in databases that are only offered to licensed personnel in the investigation industry. He, not me, was technically the only authorized user of those databases, but no one was counting. And besides, without me, my PI would most likely be manning a fry station at a fast food restaurant.

When we had a case that paid us by the hour, we were as just as quick and effective at gathering information, but in those cases, we slowed it down considerably and billed like any hourly thief does. *Why finish something now when you get paid more by finishing it later?* This is the unofficial motto of all hourly professionals.

For example, let's say we got a call on a *domestic*, which is a cheating spouse inquiry. These are typically wealthy clients and money is no object, which fit my firm perfectly as money was our only object. We charged those fat-cat clients by the hour, plus expenses. To be more specific: *by the hour* included all the hours thinking, showering, eating, masturbating, fucking, drinking, drugging, shitting, and sleeping while on the case. Expenses alone for hourly clients were a cash cow. My PI would bill the client for the expense of obtaining phone records. He would charge the client between one and two thousand dollars. My cost was either one hundred bucks to my phone company contact or we pretexted it for free. Simple supply, scam, and demand.

Plus, we knew right away if the spouse was cheating by the phone records. In fact, we knew the spouse was cheating *when* the client hired us. They all are cheating, men and women, by the time a spouse calls us in to find and gather proof. Of course, we milked those clients for upwards of ten grand before providing him or her with the proof we had in hours. Believe or not, I found rich clients actually felt better when they were charged more. I think it made them feel like the more it cost, the more extraordinary the value. Again, patience is a virtue in an hourly billing project.

Before you get angry with me again, realize your lawyer has been doing this to you for years. And your accountant. And your contractor. And your mechanic. Or someone, anyone, you pay by the hour. Even if you are friends with or related to them. At least, I admit it.[61]

Another bonus from having Uncle Sam on my staff: my licensed PI was able to testify in court. Unlike me. Why not me? Well, when you play the Kevin Bacon game with my name, it leads you right back to Uncle Louie within five moves. Not quite the background you want your expert to be asked about right after he is sworn in. Plus, there were a few *minor* charges I picked up along the way. I say *minor* because wait until you see what's coming…

Anyway, testifying in court is an hourly professional's dream. We didn't even have to pad billing in those cases when Sam was called in to testify

61 Granted, my confession comes only after I got caught scamming north of a trillion dollars, which begs the question—would I have ever come clean if I didn't get caught? The answer is: *no fucking way!* You should know by now that I would still be scamming banks, boning strippers, and vacuuming coke with my nose if I'd never gotten pinched.

because no one is in a rush in court, except the litigants paying for everything. You cannot walk into a courtroom without being delayed 20 minutes just to get through security and it costs you 200 bucks more so your lawyer could get his balls patted down.

Lawyers are the experts at convincing you they are representing your best interest. Even in the rare instances this is true, they still want your interest to be represented as slowly, with as many delays and distractions, as possible. And remember, they are not alone in scamming you. Your adversary's lawyer is conspiring with your lawyer to generate distractions, delays, problems, copies, motions, letters, and wasteful arguments.

Your lawyer will also always tell you how much they hate the other lawyer. This tactic is included in the Unofficial Lawyer's Handbook, right next to making unnecessary copies and billing you for them in the digital age. What you don't see is after the two bitter adversaries argue against each other in front of you all day in court, they meet up at the steakhouse for surf and turf. All on your tab.

Judges are in no rush either, except to retirement. They believe justice means "just not now" and they will ride your case all the way into their retirement if need be. They have no incentive to move quickly even though they are told to keep things moving by administrative judges. It's like toll collecting. Why would someone collect quickly when their reward is another vehicle, another collection? Pay a toll collector commission and there would never be traffic again. If judges were paid by the case, justice would never be delayed again. They are also tenured, but let's not get started on that.

Uncle Sam's biggest problem was that he had a hard time asking people for money. Not me. I would rob a blanket from a baby in the middle of the winter. Nevertheless, we found a way to work together using Sam as the poster boy and my covert ops runners for the dirty work.

My team really came together as a unit. My sexy secretaries were irresistible salespeople. They made our female clients comfortable with fake concern, and our male clients were convinced they had a really good chance of seeing their shaved va-jay-jays. When you put it all together with my Caller ID Jammer, our business grew exponentially. Our contacts expanded. More clients came in. Bigger clients came in. I diversified the swindles—I mean, business model— to respond to new opportunities. We went from netting hundreds each day to thousands almost seemingly overnight. And then, we started bringing in even more than that. As the money increased, so did my recycling of it right back into that night's party.

Before long, I faced growing pains. The business needed a dramatic influx of manpower just to keep up with the demand of certain clients. We were retrieving thousands of unpublished phone numbers alone. However, more people meant more risk. I didn't trust people to begin with, so I was not about to expand in the manner of a JDR-type agency. JDR had only one employee acting like Ozzy. Three hundred employees acting like Ozzy was not a sustainable venture—though let's pause and think about how fucking fun it would be to work there. That wouldn't be a business, it would be a penal colony. I would have been locked up a long time ago if I expanded through manpower. The reality was I was at the point of having to turn away easy income business simply because there was not enough time and trusted people to handle it. Then, one day I noticed a self-adhesive sticker on the office door from UPS stating "Sorry we missed you" and a line of instructions to call for re-delivery. And my deviant light bulb went off.

We had hundreds of debtors sending in overnight payments to our office on any given day. The delivery drivers became part of our family. They knew where the alcohol was in my office. They knew where the pastries were that my mother brought in. They also knew where to leave the envelopes if no one was in. So the day a sticker was left on the door, we must have gotten a new driver. The sticker he left changed my approach from individual pretexting to carpet pretexting.

With the apologetic yellow sticker in my hand, I immediately grabbed Uncle Sam and drove to Brooklyn to pay a visit with my cousin Leor, who owned a printing business. Placing the sticker on his counter, I explained to him the minor adjustments I wanted. He said fine. I told him I needed 10,000 of them. He said fine. I told them I needed them yesterday. He said to come back the next day.

The next day, I picked up the massive order and convened a meeting with my runners. We divvied up every county in New Jersey (twenty-one in total). Two teams made up of five runners would cover two counties per day. They would all wear mock UPS uniforms and travel around all day placing our brand new UPS "Sorry we missed you labels" on doors of targets we sought information on, particularly phone numbers. The runners would have to park down the block because they were not driving those shit-brown vans.

One of the minor alterations I made on our stickers was the phone number. That was left blank and written in by hand. Instead of using one number for the entire project, we wrote in a 1-800 number, then, after a week or so, we changed it to another 1-800 number. This was done because too many scams under one phone number made the number too hot to keep active.

A truly *wise* wiseguy once told me you can commit any non-violent crime, such as dealing drugs, if you do it only for three months. If you do it only for three months and then shut down and pack it up, it's almost impossible for law enforcement to have the time to learn about your operation, obtain proper warrants, investigate you, and prove you're guilty. They always prefer the ongoing criminals to the past ones as the ongoing are easier to make a case against. By the time they get wind of your activity, you're out of the game. Non-violent criminals get caught because they continue to do the same crime using the same people in the same manner. I followed that advice by committing the same crime and changing my ways, i.e., different phone numbers.

Our unsuspecting targets would come home to find our fake labels on their door and then call us to inquire about their "missed" package. The runners wrote a department store in as the sender so the targets thought they were getting a gift, not some creditor's fist up their tightwad ass. When they called in, my sweet-sounding secretaries would ask for their address. Then they placed the caller on hold and returned a minute later to apologize for the mistake and inconvenience. She would explain that the driver had accidentally placed the sticker on the wrong house. Unbeknownst to our targets, we trapped their inbound call number and sold the information to our large collection agency clients. The money poured in.

Because I was an insatiable pig when it came to cash (and pussy and coke), I decided to go further and cut out my major expense in the operation—those expensive labor costs to pay our runners to travel around the state. Plus, I needed my runners for dirtier work and there was too much of a daily risk having UPS deliverymen cruising all around towns in the middle of the day in expensive German cars. They were good at staying undetectable but like the wise wiseguy advised, it was only a matter of time before a neighbor stuck their nose in our business or a cop pulled someone over and didn't buy the story.

My solution was to turn from my Uncle Sam to your Uncle Sam for help.

The US Postal Service would unknowingly join my conspiracy for the first time (but not the last) and handle the bogus deliveries from now on. I know what you may be thinking and I was thinking the same thing—mail fraud is a federal offense and each delivery would be a new charge! But I was convinced it would bring down the risk of the operation and, honestly, I was too greedy for the cash and too successful to give a shit about getting caught.

For this rollout, I designed an official looking "Telegram" mailing. Inside was a letter from the "Sweepstakes Payout Department" with URGENT MESSAGE written across the top. It also had the name of the recipient, a 1-800 number, and a personal PIN code that they were instructed to use for their message. You've seen these before and perhaps you've even seen mine before.

Everyone who got the mailing thought Ed McMahon had been to their house to give them money. Instead, it was Ozzy McMahon in disguise showing up to *take* all your money. As soon as our subject dialed in and entered their code, our phones hung up on them. If they called us back, it hung up again. And again. Since they dialed a 1-800 number and we were paying for the call, we were entitled to the phone number information.

I called it the *trap*. Every morning, one of the girls would come in and clean out the trap. In it, there were over a hundred non-published numbers each day. It got so big, we had to start cleaning out the trap every hour.

Self-employed deadbeats were a unique challenge to us because their job information was useless. They were not about to garnish their own wages. When it came down to it, they would simply tell the court to go fuck themselves and change bank accounts. They did this routinely. They also opened new companies, whatever it took to always stay one step ahead of the collection process.

Our challenge was that we needed to grab their current and active bank account information, but they were slippery sons of bitches. *Not a problem for me!*

"Good morning, and thank you for calling Rick's Tire Service," says my slippery grease monkey target.

"Hi, this is Michael Hart with Michelin Tires in Detroit." If you don't believe me look at your Caller ID, asshole. "Can I speak with Rick Lazev?"

"This is he. How can I help you?" *It seems we have the pleasure of speaking with Deadbeat Dick—I mean, Rick—himself. Let's help him first.*

"We're having a problem processing a refund for a product recall back to your account. We attempted a bank wire twice to Rick's Tire Service at 714 Broadway in Paterson. The account we have is Kearny Bank, account number 3166171141, but it came back as undeliverable."

"That's because that account has been closed for almost a year." *No shit, shithead! Time for the bait, bitch.*

"Ah. Well, I could send you a check. Processing will be about six to eight weeks *or*—if you'd prefer, I can wire the refund to another account within 48 hours."

Rick is a suspicious dick. Don't forget he's a seasoned scammer, too. "How much is it?"

"Well, I'm not permitted to disclose the exact amount over the phone but it is classified as a jumbo check, which means it is greater than $5,000." *While Slick Rick is counting the money in his head, I slide in for the kill.* "If it's a problem, I can just submit it for processing. You'll have it by next quarter, I'm sure."

"Let me get you my *new* bank account information." *Rick is not waiting one more second for over five grand, so he gives me all his relevant bank information and soon gets four flat tires on his new business account. What a p-Rick!*

Frankly, my whole life became one continuous pretext. I wasn't sure where the line between reality and fantasy was drawn anymore. Coke doesn't clarify it very well either.

One afternoon, driving stoned down Route 17, I might have *slightly* veered off into the next lane. A horn blared and a suited man in the super-tough Pontiac Sunbird next to me went on a honking, cursing, middle-fingering rampage against me. He cut me off sharply while yelling "ASSHOLE!" and "FUCK YOU!" as he drove by. *What terrible language,* I thought to myself. Then, I looked at my watch and saw what time it was—

Fuck you time!

Keeping a close but comfortable distance behind his vehicle, I dial the New

Jersey Division of Motor Vehicles license tag number department, like I've done a hundred times before.

"License. May I help you?"

"Hi, this is Sergeant Michael Hart with the New York State Police. I need you to run a tag for me."

"What's your code, Sergeant?"

"J-082." I paid good money for all kinds of proper codes.

"Go ahead," says the cooperative DMV employee.

I state the asshole target's license plate.

"Sergeant, I show that as a silver two-door 1995 Pontiac Sunbird, registered to a Trey, with an 'e', last name Ryan at 377 Beverly Road in Glen Rock." *Bingo!*

I wrote it down while still closely following my new friend, Mr. Trey Ryan. "Okay, thank you."

I hung up and dialed 411. "I need a listing for Ryan at 377 Beverly Road in Glen Rock, New Jersey, under either Trey or the letter T."

"I have a Trey at that address; would you like to be connected?"

"Well, yes, thank you." The home phone rings and a woman answered, who hopefully is wifey.

"Hello?"

"Mrs. Ryan?" I say in my super-sweet tone.

"Yes…"

"Hi, this is Michael Hart. I'm on my way to meet Trey for a meeting. I'm on Route 17 but I'm running a little late. For some reason, I only have his home number. Would you happen to have—" She cuts me off rushing to help me and gives his cell number.

"Oh, that's wonderful. Thank you very much," I say, hanging up. That was the only statement I said so far that was true.

Now I close in on the angry T-Rey monster and see him reach down for his phone.

"Hello." He still seems a little perturbed. *Let's change his mood, shall we?*

"Yo! Fuckface!" I snap. "Who the fuck do you think you are?"

"Who's this?"

"Look in your rearview mirror, Trey Ryan from Glen Rock!"

He does and his eyes widen in fear when he looks up and sees me waving.

He's speechless. I'm not... unless you ask me to marry your daughter after sex.

"Listen to me very clearly, Trey," I growl. "Next time you stick your finger up to a stranger, you better be sure who it is."

No response. I'm now right on his tail and press, "And next time you see me on the road, pull over, and get the fuck out of my way—"

No response. I bump into his car with mine and strike terror, "If not, I will break into your fucking house at 377 Beverly Road in Glen Rock in the middle of the fucking night and fuck your wife with my glen cock in front of you. Now pull the fuck over and get the fuck out of my way!"

As I drove by him slowly, Trey Ryan from Glen Rock had his head down. The angry beast was tamed by bullshit. Nothing is tougher than bullshit.

SIXTEEN

BY THE TIME I HIT THIRTY, AFTER A MILLION HOURS LOGGED PRETEXTING—many of those hours fueled more and more by white cocoa powder—I was a self-made millionaire with a luxury condo overlooking Manhattan, a yacht docked down at the shore, luxury cars, limo and driver. My days were spent prowling for people who attempted to live financially underground while I lived the ultimate financial underground lifestyle myself. *Taxes? Don't be silly.* My nights were spent prowling nightclubs, raising hell in strip clubs, and importing tons of pussy—beautiful, exotic, strange pussy—into my apartment every night by the pound and sliced just right. I paid for all my vices and slices in cash.

Mamma Lembo, seeing my remarkable financial success, would incessantly badger me, "Now-a that-a you-a young and-a successful, why-a you no-a find-a nice-a girl-a and get-a married?"

I tried to explain to her. "But Mom, I don't like nice girls."

"What-a you-a mean, you-a no-a like nice-a girls-a?"

"I mean that nice girls, they're just not for me." What I meant, but did not quite know how to express in words to my mother, was that I wanted to keep snuffing miles of coke, downing the best champagne, and pounding strange new girls with fake names, lips, and tits up the ass just like she pounded veal cutlets. Everyone I knew who was married wanted to be me anyway, even some of the married women I was banging regularly.

During that time, there was a seismic shift in the collection industry. Too many collection agencies started breaking bad and screwing their customers over. There were too many fly-by-night competitors owned by too many scumbags. Yes, I know—I was king of the scumbags, but I was the scumbag who delivered for my customers.

Collection agencies at that time were contracted to keep anywhere from 25 to 50% of the money they collected on behalf of the clients. Apparently some of them preferred 100% of the money they collected. Then they spent it all. Then they filed bankruptcy. *Was there no honor left in the world?*

When a collection agency robbed a "collected debt", their lender-clients inherited a colossal bookkeeping nightmare trying to figure out who paid and who still owed them money. Big retailers and lenders got tired of getting screwed twice for the same debt so they stopped using third-party collection agencies like mine, and the entire collection industry bubble popped. One by one, large companies made the prudent business decision to end their bookkeeping nightmares and sever their reliance on unreliable and unethical agents.

However, large corporations were still owed millions from debtors and that debt did not just disappear off their balance sheets. It was negatively impacting their bottom lines. Remember, many of them were public companies and their uncollectible debt needed to be acceptably dealt with or their shareholders would mutiny and their stock would plummet. Their decision was to dump it. Enter Wall Street. Those boys made me look like Mother Teresa.

Companies began to compile all of their debt, i.e., charged-off accounts, for each quarter and started selling it as large "bad-debt" packages to the highest bidding investors. This is how *junk debt buyers* emerged on the financial landscape. Junk debt buyers were set up in dummy corporations by collection companies to buy bad debt. Instead of collecting debt for others and taking a commission, the collection agencies bought debt upfront for a discount (in some cases, just pennies on the dollar) using a dummy corporation. They would then collect on that debt for themselves, although on paper it was being collected for the dummy corporation.

As a result, collection agencies like mine began collecting for their own money. The large retailers and lenders (and their fat-ass shareholders vacationing on yachts in the French Rivera) were happy to be done with the debt in one line-item accounting swoop, while collection agencies now had exponentially more at stake if they failed. Basically, we had to put our own money where our lying mouths were.

The dummy corporations were necessary to avoid claims of conflict of interest. They were typically set up in the name of a friend or relative. In effect, these "owners" were another front for the collection agency. To make matters worse for debtors, when the dummy corporations purchased these junk debts, they actually—and yes, unlawfully—added their purchase price of the debt for into the actual balance. Essentially, the collection agency paid nothing for it if they were successful in collecting it, and the debtor paid even more if they ended up paying it. Of course, I piled on to that scam eventually.

This industry transition worked out great for me since I was the dirtiest player in the game. Other collection agencies, now operating as debt buyers, became my biggest customers. They now had a vested interest in the debt and were willing to pay me top dollar for information. I was getting more expensive and raking in thousands each day in profit.

Then President Clinton decided to try and fuck me.

Some old-timers remember where they were when they heard President Kennedy was shot. Others recall where they were when President Reagan got shot or when they heard that the space shuttle blew up. But a thief like me recalls exactly where I was standing, or in this case sitting (and shitting) when I heard on CNN about President Bill "Skirt Chaser" Clinton introducing his motherfucking bill HR 4943[62] which, if passed, would make it a felony to pretext financial institutions and was punishable by ten years in the slammer. *Holy shit is right, Batman!*

Through Kristy's Washington, DC, contacts, I had heard rumors about this bill (and Bill) for months, but now it was on the official legislative docket. I

---

62 Ironically, in 2002, there was another HR 4943 introduced: *The Prison Rape Reduction Act.*

couldn't believe it. Clinton was out to fuck me, too! HR 4943 was directed exclusively at information brokers who woke up every morning and stole information by phone. It should have been called the "Fuck Ozzy Bill." Worse, it had bipartisan support and was likely to pass. Sooner rather than later.

With HR 4943 on the horizon, I was forced again to reinvent my game. At the time, I was representing some of the biggest players in the collection industry from around the country. We were weeding out our small clients, i.e., nosey neighbors and crazy exes (unless they were too hot for me to turn down), and focusing exclusively on finding the most important hidden assets and bank accounts for our biggest clients. We were consistently hitting 3,000 targets a month. Things were running smoothly up until HR 4943 started to squeeze down on my tactics. To complicate the predicament, Y2K was six months away, which threatened to crash our existing computer system along with everyone else's.

Rather than bend over and let Clinton stick his burning cigar right up my ass, I doubled down on my vision. Then I doubled down again. This was not a time to consolidate or cut my losses. I was not about to run for cover. My coke habit was getting more, not less, expensive. While my pussy-ass peers were already licking their wounds over the impending legislation, I was plotting to take over the motherfucking world.

I just needed to build a better mousetrap.

Every collection attorney who did business in the State of New Jersey was basically a regular client. We would provide to them an *asset locate* and/or skip-trace on their debtors, which is primarily banking and employment information, which they then used to execute judgments. The difference with my company was that our policy for these big clients was "No Find, No Fee." If I didn't locate any assets, they wouldn't have to pay me a dime. Other services charged per search because they sucked at searching. To use me didn't cost them anything unless I scored—much like personal injury attorneys, I was working on a contingency fee basis. And the one thing about attorneys is that if you can save them money, they will love you. Make them money, and you can fuck their wife.

Here's how it goes down: my collection attorney clients provide me lists, paper or electronically, of their active judgments with no recent activity. For every account or judgment they send me, I send it back having located either a bank account, employment information, or both. The client then pays me an agreed upon fee per hit.

The problem now was, with President Clinton's hard-on for me (and his interns), I had to come up with a way to be able to continue to retrieve massive amounts of information *without* pretexting.

The solution was not immediate. It took me weeks of analyzing and considering a bunch of different options. In reality, I was always thinking of a better and cheaper way to conduct my scams, but now I was being forced to or lose much of my business. The solution, it turns out, was under my nose the whole time. *No, it was not cocaine!*

I already had a nice stable of inside bank tellers who trusted me and were there to look things up for me whenever necessary, but I was not utilizing them in an organized and efficient manner. To benefit from them, I needed to spend my precious time calling them all the time or visiting with them just to track one or two targets.[63] I would also have to buy them a gift card or buy dinner in exchange for their assistance. Too much heavy lifting for me. Too much waste. Not efficient enough for the big time.

I now needed wider, deeper, and quicker access to sensitive databases that no one else had. Replicating anything on a larger scale is always a challenge, especially for crime. To stay successful in the game, I needed a better organized team of corrupt insiders following set protocols. The objective became to communicate targets to insiders in a standardized manner, have them conduct standardized searches, have them deliver back hits in a standardized way, and pay them a standardized fee. This situation wasn't for everyone. I was not about to have an army of bankers fall in love with me to win over their trust and favors. This was a new level of cooperation and compensation. My cash would buy all the trust I needed. If you had the time and the balls, then Ozzy had the cash to make your participation worthwhile.

My vision extended beyond banks to insiders embedded anywhere information was a commodity. I needed moles burrowing for me in credit unions, healthcare offices, state agencies, federal labor departments, etc. They had to have the clearance and authority to punch in a subject's social security number (which is the key identifier in the financial world) into their respective

---

63 All bank insider exchanges flowed directly through me because I trusted no one to handle my tellers directly.

database and provide me with all current records pertaining to a target.

The critical component is *current* information. The past was useless to my clients, hence useless to me. Finding jobs or place of business locates were already easy enough for me. My New Jersey Department of Labor contacts were deep and they had access to a database that, with a social security number, could find if a subject was working. Current employment data was still a few months behind as the state had records pertaining to employers filing wages, which was done on a quarterly, not weekly or a monthly, basis. However, most of the time the information unlawfully obtained from my insiders was current enough to be classified and paid as a hit.

Another route we already had covered was health insurance. Those providers had all your employment information in their computer system because benefits were deducted from an individual's paycheck for health insurance, such as BlueCross BlueShield or Aetna. A bonus offered from our health insurance insiders was they also offered private, privileged health information on targets. That information was rarely requested, but when it was requested, it was sold for big bucks and I think I just gave you another reason to hate your insurance company.

But back to banking. Current banking information was the most difficult to locate. Labor and healthcare information could be found for millions of people by searching just one source. However, there were literally hundreds of potential banks just in my county that may have an account with any given individual. With one insider only capable of searching information for one specific financial institution, my bank searches were a crapshoot. My new vision was to break the bank wide open. To do that, I allocated a half million in bribes and upfront money. As it turns out, it was only half of what I ending up needing.

My new strategy first needed another front. By now, I had so many, what was one more? This one needed to be a physical criminal headquarters that was not my office and fitting to my vision. I turned to the place I felt most at home since I left my mother's womb. Strip clubs!

Strip clubs aren't for everyone, but they are for me. It turns out they were for most people I dealt with also. So like any good businessman, I located my headquarters to meet the needs and demands of my market (and my penis). My new command center was opened unofficially in Satin Dolls, a strip club located only one mile from my home that appropriately doubled as *Bada Bing!*

for the TV show *The Sopranos*. My good friend "Tony" owned a piece of the place so I had carte blanche, and of course I was already a fixture. Satin Dolls was the ideal place to close my high-end clients and insiders using some of the finest high-end rear ends in the northeast. Satin Dolls oozed money, women, and drugs. It was already home to a lot of society's well-off parasites and it became home sweet home to me, too.

Strippers were a big piece of the equation, but they were not enough. My new approach and vision needed the proper equipment, a sophisticated computer system, and infrastructure capable of supporting and tracking thousands of illicit transactions each month. Problem was the system I was imagining did not exist. Nor did the scope of the crimes I was envisioning, for that matter. Problem number two was Y2K was counting down, stressing out the whole world. Of course, I was planning to launch right after Y2K hit. Just to keep it interesting.

During that time, you may recall, computer crash rumors were so exaggerated that people actually believed it would bring about apocalyptic doom. Some people were actually making preparations to survive like Kevin Costner in *Waterworld*. To most survivors, that would be a better fate than watching that shit movie. In any event, I prepared for the worst by calling in the best, my Russian comrades.

The good news for me was they arrived on time. The good news for them they were also drunk. Who the hell wakes up in the morning and starts drinking? Russians, that's who![64] We sat down and I blueprinted for them my entire vision. The system I was envisioning would have to be so advanced that it would make Steve Jobs feel like a complete failure in life. Once they scoped it out, they told me they wanted a year to finish it and two hundred grand; I gave them four months and two fifty. One thing about communists: they love money way more than capitalists. I already knew the drill. A steady stream of vodka and Red Bull was required. For me, it would be a steady stream of coke and Diet Coke.

While the Reds went right to work on my new computer system, I turned my attention to developing more clients and contacts. One of my first big closes was one of the head constables for the State of New Jersey. Enlisting him into my growing stable of deceit was huge. When attorneys called him to garnish wages of debtors, seize funds, or attach chattel, he told them to call me. It was his official duty to collect as a court officer and he steered clients right into

---

64 Imagine what these guys could have created sober! Then again, maybe they were better and more creative when wasted, like The Beatles.

my lap because I could do it better than him or anyone. Well, that's not really why he sent me clients. He did it because of the greenery I planted back on his lap and the fact that my girls gave new meaning to his title head constable whenever he stopped in.

I put together a master list of every agency, bank, and company that I wanted to infiltrate and began working on expanding my customer base. Please do not get the impression that I was doing all the legwork myself. I had many people working for me at the time and over the years. Too many to mention, really. A true crime book is not one where you thank all your cronies. Interestingly, almost all of them were spared criminal prosecution, which makes them all fortunate. It also makes them all suspects against me.

Anyway, if my forecast of numbers was correct, one contact per bank location was not enough. Three was my objective. I contacted everyone I knew and cast the word out far and wide as to my specific needs. You may be wondering why the dramatic change in approach from a careful, calculated Ozzy so concerned with trust to the bold and brash Ozzy sending out loud recruiting calls while waving bundles of cash? The answer is simple. Cocaine.

You may also be pondering to yourself that if you were in my shoes at that time and you had made millions in the shadows, you probably would have packed up and gone to an island. Rather than roll the dice more, why not quit while way ahead and live comfortably off a very lucky run for the rest of my life? The answer is simple. Cocaine. *She don't lie...she don't lie...she don't lie.*

It was well known that if anyone introduced me to an insider and I enlisted that insider into my operation, they were five grand richer just for the introduction. My marketing was similar to Amway, only it was immoral and far more lucrative. You would be surprised how many introductions get thrown your way when you dangle five grand in cash from your strip club office. It was not long before the top-earning stripper in the house enlisted in my new venture.

Dina was seductively beautiful. Dark smooth skin, cat eyes, dark flowing hair, and "best in show" tits. She was the best recruiter, ever. Period. Girls trusted her. Guys loved her. She loved money and knew how to make it...or should I say take it. Not just for me. From me! A lesson I would learn the hard way down the road.

Meanwhile, I had Uncle Sam on the road meeting with every collection agency and law firm from Bergen County to Cape May. With his PI license in one hand and a DRL contract in the other, Sam signed them up en masse, until there was virtually no one left to recruit. We promised to deliver more than anyone in the information business ever had. And we only had to be paid if we were successful. It was an offer they couldn't refuse.

With Sam as head of sales, my office staff running operations, my Ruskies in information technology, and Dina in charge of public relations, I remember feeling that I actually appeared legit and almost felt legit. *Almost* was good enough for a guy who hadn't been legit since he delivered newspapers on a bicycle. Then, I looked around and saw all the strippers on my payroll and looked down at the lines of snow on the table below me and snapped right back to my beautiful, crazy reality.

The next phase was recruiting the insiders. I had done this all my life, focusing mostly on banks, but I needed to get many more insiders into my network and place them into a very smooth system of operations and compensation in a short amount of time. Between my contacts, Dina's network, and the contacts sent over by Uncle Louie,[65] I had a large list of prospects coming in. One by one, I pitched them on making a little extra money on the side. When it comes to business, Italians believe in peace. What I mean is everyone needs a *piece*. My track record in that department was impeccable. I was educated by the streets to pay myself last. Everyone always made money with me.

Here again, as before, my other advantage was bank tellers are a predominately female field. When it came to pleasure, I was picky about women. Okay, you know enough about me by now so I'll qualify that—when I was sober and… well, not really even then. Anyway the point is when it came to business, I was never picky. I'll admit some were minnows and others were whales, but business is business and I was a master at mixing pleasure with business. I didn't have the time to schmooze them over weeks, besides my recruiters already laid the groundwork so the in-person "interview" would be all about presenting my high-society world as theirs for the taking.

Criminal seduction is most commonly achieved by dangling and then delivering cash. Sometimes I sprinkled in drugs and sex to close a deal when circumstances demanded. For the ladies, I still made sure each felt a spiritual connection with me—which was, as usual, based on a complete pile of bullshit I fed them about our similarities during my accelerated courting. Whether

---

65 He may have kicked me out of the mob, but he didn't stop earning some quick cash off my enterprise.

we were sleeping together or not, every woman was made to feel unique and special. They were my personal partners in life. And crime. *Togetherness: isn't that what crime is all about?*

My expertise in banking combined with my lies about my feelings toward them earned me a close rate of almost 100%. Those who didn't take me up on my offers would often pass me on to someone who would play ball, and grabbed five grand for themselves for that intro. The bottom line was all of them needed the extra money—I never met anyone in my life that didn't need extra money—that Big Ozzy offered, and some of them needed the comfort of Little Ozzy in their life, too. When Big and Little Ozzy worked together in perfect harmony—that was a thing of beauty. And lots of dirty, filthy sex. And tons of coke.

SEVENTEEN

ONCE I CLOSED AN INSIDER PROSPECT, WE CUT IMMEDIATELY TO THE BRASS TACKS of the deal. We went over our arrangement in detail, how to use the software, how to get in the system, how to get out of the system, and to never, ever manipulate the target account or any account. *Just like you are supposed to do when you go camping or hiking: leave no trace!*

To get hired at a bank at that time, there were only two customary requirements: you could not have a criminal record and you could not have bad credit. Having a brain was not a requirement to work at a bank. I frankly think they preferred the dimwits. To commit crimes at a bank on my behalf, however, you had to have at least half a brain. Banks used to place a great deal of emphasis on their employee's financial health. Today I believe they are prohibited by law from discriminating based on bad credit, but back then they would reject you if you had large debts or bad credit. Although you were not a convicted criminal, banks assumed if you were in a desperate financial situation that you were a risk to be one. The good girls the banks hired became criminals the second they printed out one piece of paper containing personal account information for me. To them, it didn't feel like a stickup and a high-speed getaway, but in effect, that was exactly how the law viewed it.

What was in it for them to engage in such conduct? Twenty bucks cash per hit. *Doesn't seem like much, eh?* Believe me, it added up quickly. A hit was a bank account number and balance for any target on my collection list. The teller girls had the security clearance, plus anonymity, invisibility, and speed.

Back at my new "office", Dina was an unstoppable feeder. She started approaching and recruiting branch managers and vice presidents. She brought the male ones into the club where they enjoyed VIP treatment in the VIP room. There was no need to seduce the men with my bullshit. I had them at hello. And they came back regularly to get paid, laid, and wasted, all compliments of yours truly. Dina must have made six figures in cash just for the introductions alone. Did I try to sleep with her? Yes—every single time I saw her... just like everyone else did. Just like you would. Even if you were married. Check that—*especially* if you were married. Didn't I describe how juicy and titillating her tits were? Or how flat her stomach was? Or how fucking jacked up and perfect her ass was? And her pierced bellybutton and paw print tattoos running up her thigh…

Sorry, but I need to stop there 'cause I cannot describe her any further without chubbing up. Not that I'm anti-chub now, it's just that I'm in the worst place in the world right now to chub. My roommate would tell you I'm in the best place to chub, but he's slated to be here much longer than I am. Don't get me wrong; he's a cool dude to talk to and I wish I could share my chub with him, but honestly you couldn't sketch an uglier person, male or female. Nice guy, but his face could turn a lifetime prisoner straight.

But Dina "resisted" me—which was an easier word for my ego to cope with than "rejected". No worries, mate. History proved no one who hung around me long enough was able to resist me forever. This may sound like I'm bragging, but I'm not bragging. I am stating a fact. Not because I was the Fonz with the ladies, but because if you hung around me you were constantly surrounded by hardcore drugs, drinking, and deviant sexual behaviors. There was simply no way to be a part of the Ozzy crazy train and remain apart from it. The way Dina resisted is she simply stayed away from me entirely, except for when we were handling business. In retrospect, I should have stayed away from her like she was a prosecutor. Or a rat. Or King Kong.

✦ ■ ✦

Months of legwork were complete. Contacts were in place, trained, and ready to hit the ground running. State labor personnel, healthcare insurance agents, and every bank on my list was covered A-to-Z. I categorized each contact into one of three teams, either A, B or C. I wanted a quick way of telling me everyone's value with one letter on my screen. In the beginning, team classification was determined primarily by job position. Later, it was determined by results. For example, contacts that worked at banks and held senior job titles, such as Manager or Vice President, were enlisted into the A-team. Assistants or those due for a promotion were on the B-team. Entry-level tellers were placed on the C-team, though some ended up being as valuable as the A-team. The classifications were fluid. People were promoted and moved up a team, some moved up or down based upon performance, others dropped out. Employment contacts in state departments automatically received and stayed as A-team classification due to their positioning and authority over such a high volume.

The time for talking and planning was over. It was time to deliver. My new fat cat customers were hungry for real results, not promises. The only issue was the software. Everything, I mean, EVERY-FUCKING-THING, hinged on implementing a platform of user-friendly, effective, covert software. If my technology didn't deliver, I was ruined.

Luckily, my Russian comrades came through like they did at Stalingrad. They designed a fucking amazing system. Thirteen computers in total. My skip trace system was better than having R2D2 work for me. It detailed every debtor that was entered into my database and was able to predict everything, from probability to geography. It analyzed the closest banks to a target's home and the closest banks to their job. It even was able to provide details on the nearest pizza joint and the nearest Home Depot should we get a tip one of our targets worked there.

They also created a program called *Watchdog*, a monitoring system that was linked with the three major credit reporting agencies and would send me daily emails advising me if one of my subjects had some type of credit activity such as looking to purchase a car or inquiring about a mortgage. We were ahead of the times and crimes!

This brilliant system organized and manipulated all the data I needed for the massive undertaking I envisioned. As an information crook, the thing

I love most about technology is that it cuts down on people and that means less expense, but most importantly, less risk, just like when I introduced the fax machine to Uncle Louie's operation. Sure, I now had a large network of unstable humans employed, but the system and procedures they followed were so simple and undetectable it actually *decreased* the chance of getting caught.[66] Going over my new system, I knew my crazy vision was actually within reach. Shit—I felt like Lex Luthor, Criminal Collection Genius. I gave my Red friends a bonus as a sign of my appreciation: two of the best hookers from my stable and two 8-balls each. They slept for a week straight.

My daring, new business venture and ballooning coke habit were making me increasingly paranoid like Scarface, so I also had the Russians install video monitors throughout my condo that linked into my work computers. Now I had a state-of-the-art, pimped out computer system with monitors/TVs everywhere, including the bathrooms. I had cameras in the parking lot. Cameras in the hall. Cameras outside the building. Management must have thought security installed the cameras. Security must have thought management installed them to make sure they weren't sleeping or jerking off on the job. And my neighbors must have felt their dues were being well spent to keep them safe.

The multi-room monitor system was also great for the true love of my life, the only love that never leaves you: porn. Over years of practice and intense training, I was finally a full-fledged, kinky-as-fuck freak and a steady diet of porn was essential to maintain this accomplishment. In order to meet my appetite and demands, my porn collection was diverse and perverse. We won't say how diverse and perverse. Let's just say the detectives must have enjoyed watching what actually goes on at some barnyards when they confiscated my hard drive.

I never had a relationship turn stale sexually, and this was probably because I was never monogamous, even for a night. But I would advise anyone who has lost the spice to tap into the magical world of porn before you pay a therapist. Always choose a theme and style that fits your partner's frame of mind, not mine, or you will probably send her running to the police. Believe me, I have learned that the hard way. *Never show before you know* is the golden rule of smut film therapy.

Forget counseling and follow your Dr. Oz's romantic advice—mix in a little

66 In hindsight, maybe *delayed* is a better word to use.

porn spice and I promise before long you will have a collection of toys and cuffs... or a divorce. Either way, you won't have to waste time in therapy. If lucky, you may even get to introduce another participant to the party. Playing *Match the Porn* is my favorite way to spend quality time together with my friends. I highly recommend it. Just be daring and be creative. Think outside of the box. All boxes.

For example, most guys like to tie someone up, do their dirty deed, untie their sex captive, and hit the showers. Not Ozzy. That shit is weak! Shower? After I "finish" all over my captive, she don't get no stinkin' shower. At that point, I would reach over to the bondage restraints and—just when my little hostage slut was thinking about her freedom and wet naps—tighten the ropes more. Now that is real domination. Trust me with this one. It's an incredible turn-on for both prisoner and warden. Just get an advance waiver signed.

After your slave is more firmly restrained, you need to leave. Not just the room, the residence. That's correct: walk out the door, get in your car, and drive away. I liked picking up dry cleaning or running a few errands. My favorite was to return with another satin doll.

"Honey, we're home…"

Just one piece of advice: make sure you are the first person to return. My cleaning lady was never the same again.

I don't want to leave out my single students reading this who can't even get a girl to kiss them, let alone afford the company of a bondage hooker. Lucky for you, I'm also an equally accomplished expert in self-sex. Masturbation, you already know, is critical to achieving personal enlightenment and gratification whether you're single or coupled. Don't take my word for it—science has proven no one can touch your pleasure pickle like yourself, except the Asian masseuses on Astoria Boulevard in Queens. But whether or not you ever get to Queens, you should never feel ashamed. Masturbation, I'm certain, is the reason why the divorce rate is not 100% so I encourage all my readers to "embrace" it. Do it now. Right now. This book can wait thirty seconds…

To truly *mastur* your domain, it goes without saying you need a good imagination. And pornography offers the best pathway to new, imaginary pleasure adventures, like banging Jenna Jameson; or bestiality, like banging Ron Jeremy. I believe every one of my readers has what it takes to become a masturful masturbator like me. You just need to put your hands to it. I heard it takes 10,000 hours of practice to mastur something, which means I was done practicing by the age of 21. Truth be told, three times a day was common for me at the peak of my work stress, sexual prime, and drug abuse. Wait. That's a lie. It's still common for me. This was in addition to the steady stream of multi-whore sex I indulged in. Long before the government labeled me *mastermind*, I had labeled myself "masturmind." You can do it, too!

EIGHTEEN

ON DECEMBER 31, 1999, THE WORLD WAS READY TO END AND MY LAUNCH WAS ready to go. Data was entered into my new system. The backup was in place. The waiting game was coming to an end and every minute felt like an hour to me. By now, I'd invested over a million dollars in finder's fees, hardware, software, and bribes. Double what I had initially projected. I was all in on this and then some. My conspirators were in all the right places. The more-than-a-million-dollar question remaining was: *would it still work after Y2K?*

That New Year's Eve was a blur of a bunch of strippers, my two Russians, a semi-conscious Marty, and a blizzard of coke. Honestly, that was what many nights back then were like for me. But that night, as the clock struck twelve and the ball in Times Square dropped, so did my balls in fear of ruination.

Then, suddenly, the world did not end. There were no power outages, no computer crashes, and no shutdowns of the world order. Kevin Costner was still alive and making shit movies. Doomsday, so it seemed, would have to wait.

For now, my chaotic world, which was way more chaotic than a normal person could possibly imagine, was in order. It was all I could've asked for. It was everything I strove for. I remember swelling with pride.[67] Excitement. Hope. It was the new millennium, a new chapter, and I was pumped and ready for the big time.

I was also a hardcore coke addict.

My cocaine consumption had been keeping me jacked up all day and night. I had two speeds: fast and faster. Days were spent in my office, nights at Satin Dolls. Ayeda, Jenna, Laura, Elissa, Shira, Jessica, Banana, Fanna, and Foe Fanna… why have one stripper, when you can have three? Did I say five? Like wiseguys, I gave my strippers nicknames, which objectified them further, such as "The Leaning Towers of Lisa" or "My-Oh-Maya." We would all party into the next day, five to six days each week. No one had the stamina to participate every night, except me. I was the center of all the mayhem, the master of all the ceremonies. Every party, every night.

But cocaine makes everyone a slave, including me. Like any vice, it is a slow progression, and you don't notice anything different until that one moment when it hits you and it's too late. For me, it was the last minute of 1999 that I realized I had crossed the line from party-guy to hardcore addict just like that.[68] *How in the fuck did this happen to me*, I asked myself. I was too shrewd for this slavery, too strong to be unwillingly captive. Ozzy was a boss. Ozzy used coke. Coke didn't use Ozzy. When the reality set in, I spent the next couple of hours feeling confused, then angry, then upset, then sorry for myself. Then back to angry again. I cried. I screamed.

Ultimately, I vouched to fix it. I was the fixer of everything. Everyone came to me to fix their problems. I answered to nothing and no one. A final proclamation was issued loudly inside my head to dial back my use. *So let it be written, so let it be done.* My use had gone too far for too long. The time had come to *stop* the abuse!

And this resolution I'd made, it made me speed up. Way up. I did more and more cocaine trying to do less and less of it. What an evil, vicious, merciless drug I was addicted to. Readers, make a mental note.

Coke started out as a valuable tool. It served my lifestyle, my work, and the

---

67 Little Ozzy swelled with pride, too.

68 Of course, others knew this for years and you've probably known this for chapters.

company I was keeping. It enabled me to work around the clock. On it, I always thought bigger. I was braver. It enhanced my party personality. I rewarded my cohorts with it. It elevated my sexual encounters. Cocaine was the perfect additive for the character "Ozzy." I felt alive, acutely alert, focused. Then, once addiction kicked in, I only felt torture, agony, and pain. With or without it.

If you have never tried cocaine, don't. I repeat, DO NOT! There is no sarcasm to my words; there is no humor in my voice. There are tears in my eyes as I tell you this.

Please heed my advice. If you don't want to listen to a lowlife like me, I totally understand, but look at my life for your evidence of what cocaine does. Your first line will deliver an incredible euphoric feeling that lasts an hour or so. Then when you come down, it's complete hell. In that one flashing moment, the drug takes over your mind and doesn't let go, sometimes for days. Your feelings go from euphoric to being singularly fanatical about chasing the original high you had just a short time ago. That original high, however, will never come back. I promise you. I chased it down as long and as hard as anyone who ever survived to tell about it. And that is the tragic, tortuous irony of the drug— by the time you feel its greatest high, you are automatically and permanently incapable of ever feeling that way again.

Once addicted, you will start to do all kinds of stupid shit, from cleaning your apartment nineteen times to endlessly gazing out the window. Those are innocent compulsions. They're not all innocent. Inevitably, cocaine will make you violent toward those around you, even those who you care about the most. This is why I call it the devil's dust. And naturally, you do more to forget the guilt. It will conceal your sense of caution. You'll want all kinds of crazy sexual adventures, but the "little guy" refuses to cooperate because you did too much. So you do more to cope.

But wait. It gets worse.

Paranoia sets in. Once you reach this point, you get dog hearing. It seems like you can hear a door slam from six blocks away. At its sinister worst, especially for a man in my line of work, your mind convinces you "they" are coming. All of them. A whole army of them. You have no fucking idea who "they" are, but you're absolutely positive that they're about to kick down your door before your next eye blink. You do more coke to deal with these boogiemen fears and the more you do, the more boogiemen there are. *Fuck me!*

At the dawn of the new millennium, with the largest breach of privacy machine in history primed and ready to go, I unknowingly signed up for the cocaine torture installment plan that would last the next six years and ultimately bring me down from criminal heaven to criminal hell.

I believe it was the great American philosopher George Carlin who said that cocaine makes you want to do more cocaine. My life proved his theory.

And enough with the buzzkill part of the story. Let's get back to business.

My million-dollar investment and vision paid off immediately. *Whew!* DRL went from doing a thousand hits a week to ten thousand a month. My business transformation from pretexting to working directly on the inside blew away my competitors. While bank security departments were focusing on armed robbers, check scams, and chaining down their fucking pens, I zeroed in on a far more valuable, less assuming commodity—information. And I had built a better mousetrap to get it. *Thank you, Mr. President, for the inspiration!*

Since the new computer system was working just fine, I took the old one with the old data and stored it someplace safe. Just in case.[69] And, as my clients slept like babies, I barely slept at all. The excitement of the new business possibilities dominated my mind. After the first three months, I did a comparison study with my competitors. It showed DRL outscored our competition sixteen to one. This meant that for every other asset locator and/or pretexter in the business who successfully located one asset, we located sixteen. *Sixteen, bitches!*

I was on track to have the best year ever. I could not spend all the money or fuck all the pussy.[70] I started calling every girl *Bella*[71] because I could not remember all their names. Abortions became a line item on my personal budget. Every night at 2am, I closed down Satin Dolls and brought the party home. I purchased all kinds of fancy toys for myself and showered my friends and girlfriends with trips and gifts galore. Coke was part of my regular groceries. It was delivered direct to my house every week by my Colombian pharmaceutical rep.

I was stuffing safe deposit boxes all around New Jersey. I hid money everywhere: in speakers, closets, behind the wall, under the floor, suitcases, even at my friends' houses. I hid so much money in so many different places

---

69 FYI: The government never found my old computers.

70 And believe me, I tried really hard!

71 *Bella* means beautiful in Italian.

that I forgot where it was after a while. If I visited your house regularly during those days, there is a good chance I stashed money in your basement. If I could have back just *half* the money I hid over those years and forgot where, I would be writing this story from a Central American beach resort instead of from inside a monkey cage in New Jersey.

Did I invest? You bet I did. I put the money out on the street through an old Uncle Louie contact for seven points per week. He kept two points in exchange for keeping me out of it entirely. You can't say I ever forgot my roots.

How did my cronies do? My good bank contacts made thirty to a hundred thousand, plus benefits at their legit "day job." Working for me, they added an extra sixty to one hundred thousand grand in cash, depending on their results. My payoffs and organizational structure was a true meritocracy. Now keep in mind they made that extra money by clicking a few key strokes during their "day job."

It was interesting to witness what my contacts did with their *side* cash every week. The prudent ones banked their entire paycheck and lived off the cash. Others bundled the cash into rolls of thousands and hid it all around their house. One paid for his brother's college. Most of the guys hid it from their wives and blew it all on women and drugs. Some ladies did the same.

Like any business, there were occasions I needed to replace an insider due to maternity leave,[72] laziness, ineffectiveness, rehab, or moving away. It should be noted that none, *not one ever*, walked away saying their conscience just couldn't take it anymore. Money is its own morality. Whatever the case, I was always on the prowl for new contacts. Of course, I had to profile these contacts before I hired them to profile for me. After I unlawfully ran motor vehicle, credit, and background checks, I would know exactly how dirty their underwear was before I approached them. I suspect I was the only criminal enterprise that did background checks on my accomplices to see if they were a proper fit and profile to commit acts of ill repute. Once I zeroed in on a new prospect, I—or if you were a male, Dina—would "run" into you. Getting coffee. At the car wash. In the gym. Soon you were out to lunch or dinner with one of us, and then, before you realized what happened, you were giving me a hit or two. Then, you were giving me a thousand hits.

I had a few *floaters* in my stable to call in, too. A floater was a bank contact with extensive bank experience that could and would get hired at a specific

72 The kid was not mine, I swear!

bank once we knew a merger was imminent such as when First Union merged with Wachovia or Fleet Bank merged with Bank of America. They all possessed stellar resumes and were usually hired on the spot. Good for them, but even better for me. With all the levies these banks were getting hit with, I often wondered how not one dickhead in the banks' internal loss prevention offices ever caught wind of my scent. No doubt they were racking in overtime hours and not noticing anything fishy whatsoever. *Zzzzzzzzz......*

One contact was a shooting star right from the beginning. Her name was Candy. She was my white trash, wonder woman when it came to finding bank accounts. She was the only teller for a remote branch of Fleet Bank up in Sussex County, New Jersey—in other words, hillbilly country. *Cue up the banjo!* Anyway my Candy girl, like me, was a big fan of the almighty dollar. Her branch was an actual trailer. That's right! It was a trailer branch. Being in the sticks, it was never busy with customers so Candy had plenty of time to troll for my targets. We had a very successful partnership and she was unabashed in wanting me to bang her like a broken screen door in a hurricane. I, of course, wanted to, but this is the one woman that I just couldn't.

I realize that was the most impossible line to believe in this book, but poor Candy was the true definition of a *butterface*. Great body, *but her face!* Her body was a legit eight or nine[73], but her face looked like the mold for gorilla cookies. And that gorilla played hockey. Goalie, without a mask. I called it *summer teeth*—some are here, some are there. And teeth, or lack thereof, was my sexual repellent. I laid my pipe for all shapes, sizes, and all kinds of fugly creatures but I had one rule: good teeth. Or maybe it was just they had to have most teeth. I can't tell you a specific number of teeth needed, but it was certainly more teeth than the amount in Candy's mouth.

I wanted to be her tooth fairy by sending her to my cousin who was a dentist. Ultimately, I decided against it because I was actually afraid she would take offense and sever our booming partnership. Before you judge, I could easily look beyond her face, if she just fixed her teeth. Remarkably, Candy was my reigning insider champ, loved to party, and was very horny, and yet still we did not copulate. Not even once. Week after week, Candy consistently landed over 200 hits. She was a hit machine. The Pete Rose of my operation. One day, when the snow kept the trailer park customers away, she sat alone all day in the branch and collected 304 fucking hits. An all-time, single day record that will

73 I've fucked twos before, seriously. Every five of them equaled a ten.

never be beat.[74]

One week, Candy came down personally to my office to pick up her earnings for that week. *Enough was enough!* I had been with awful looking women before and it was time for me to get over my fears and shag this chick like she wanted. I psyched myself up with a cocktail of bong hits and coke. I put on The Doors. Little Ozzy told me he was ready to serve his master. It had a chance, I swear. I looked down and focused down when she walked in. She smelled nice, which is very helpful. She had short jean shorts on, which was sexy. Okay, the white Reebok high tops were from another era, but the legs were in good shape. Little Ozzy was getting ready and even commenced preparation inflation. Then, it happened. *Fuck!* To this day, I regret it. I made the deadly mistake of looking up—which was not a deal breaker in itself—and then Candy smiled ear-to-ear when I held out her six grand in cash. Little Ozzy saw the two or three Chiclets, flattened out, and retreated like a scared turtle.

I paid Candy and hugged her goodbye.

---

74 I hate to give away the ending, but the business is closed now.

NINETEEN

MY SUCCESSFUL INSIDER-BRIBING STRATEGY BEGS THE QUESTION, "Why didn't I just bribe from the beginning?" The answer is simple. Back when I first started in the game, there were too many banks to tap. Then the big banks began to buy out all the little banks. Mergers and buyouts contributed to a boom in the banking business. It also unintentionally boomed my business, as I was able to do much more searching and cover much more ground with far fewer insiders. For me, the opportunities widened with mergers and buyouts while my risk actually narrowed. Back in my pretexting days, my inventory consisted of less than 20,000 accounts, compared to the millions of placements I was bringing in after the millennium.

In the year 2001, DRL raked in over ten million bucks. Our new President George *dub-you* Bush signed HR 4943 into law as soon as he finished unpacking his underpants in the White House. It was now less of a crime to club endangered baby seals in a public square than to pretext a billion dollar financial institution for information.

My number one associate, Dina, was also raking in the loot but she still refused to participate in my after-hours debauchery. Unlike the rest of my honey money bunnies, she just took the money and left. I knew that she had a boyfriend, but as long as she kept her silicone team in line, I didn't give a fuck what or who she did after work as long as she produced. Like me, Dina knew how to spread the cash around so that it came back around to her and me again and again.

Meanwhile, I was making my clients richer than myself. A couple of the nation's largest debt buyers were making so much money they decided to go public on the stock exchange. *Now ain't that the motherfucker of all fronts?* Were they my clients? Of course they were, through a maze of subsidiaries and partnership fronts riding the Ozzy crazy, gravy train.

In a hypercompetitive field, I did what any other good Italian man in my position would do—I wiped out my competition. Not by force, but by finesse. In doing so, I was approached by many other firms nationwide trying to attach their train cars to my train. The entire industry was huge, but it was controlled by a surprisingly small amount of people. No more than a hundred nationwide and I was one of the two top collectors in the country because of our accuracy.

The industry would meet several times a year all across the country at conventions, workshops, and seminars. It was a chance for everyone to get away from bitchy wives (or husbands) and bratty kids and party like they were Keith Moon... or Ozzy Lembo. My peers and I were like a family of thieves. We partied together, worked together, and shared some of our best secrets to liberate cash from debtors across the country together. Most importantly, we helped mitigate our risk together and increase our returns together through too many schemes to mention...without implicating some of my old associates. Perhaps, one day, I will change my mind and start naming real names when I leave this shithole and find out for sure who pointed fingers at me. *Nervous, anyone?* I would be. Ozzy will return. And he may be coming for you, so whatcha gonna do?

◆ ◼ ◆

In those days, state law enforcement personnel were the ones we all had to look out for. They licensed private investigators and did everything they could to discredit, or worse, set them up. Some of their motivation was certainly ego-driven, which I can relate to just a little bit. They thought they were the only true investigators. The way they would sting you was to pose as a potential new client and come in with a list of fake targets that they were requesting information on. Then, the police would sit back and watch how we obtained the information as they red-flagged all these fake participants in all the databases across a state. I must admit their approach was savvy. It also posed zero threat for my operation.

First of all, I was already paying some of the same cops who were charged with stinging people like me. Further, I never entertained any mysterious new clients looking for information. In that sense, and only that sense, I kept my nose clean.

By this time, my collectability percentage *exceeded* a mind-blowing 65%. Industry standard was *less* than ten percent. So now you know why everyone wanted a piece of me. DRL was scrubbing each and every account thoroughly and no one could compete, especially in my area of the country.

Here's how we scrubbed for millions of dollars:

Scrubbing meant taking each target and running them through my contacts at every single bank, starting from the largest (Bank of America) to the smallest (trust companies, back then) and every bank in between. One-by-one, my targets' social security numbers were entered into these sensitive databases. If a match was found, it was immediately reviewed to determine whether or not it was still valid. Valid meant it was open and not an ITF (in trust-for a/k/a custodial account) or an IRA.[75] If the account came in as valid, the contact either hit the print screen or wrote down the account number(s) together with the balance to avoid the scrutiny of a shared printer.

They were also trained to write down the work contact number listed on the account. This way, in the matter of a simple phone call, I could couple a *bank hit* with a *wage hit*,[76] provided that the job information was current. Not only did it save time, it also saved me money by eliminating a later bribe or pretext.

As the list was placed from bank to bank, targets whose accounts were located from the previous bank had their name removed from the list. Hence, the list got smaller for each successive bank contact to process as targets were removed. Let's say between Bank of America and Wachovia we got back hits

---

75 The reason we checked for ITF and IRA account designations is those types of bank accounts were exempt from being levied.
76 And a *bong hit*, too.

on 25% of the target list. When the list was passed to Commerce and PNC Bank, it went from 1,000 names down to 750 names. You see why I started with the largest banks—because they carried more likelihood of target hits. After each list was run through every bank in the top ten markets then, and only then, would we pass it over to the smaller institutions. Efficiency. Expediency. Cost effectiveness. That's how you break the law properly.

Once we scrubbed the banks, it went it to our job guys, who were responsible for running the remaining names into their state database. As with the banks, the hit needed to be checked for validity. An old job was helpful but not a commodity for me to sell. As mentioned, jobs were also the least timely data as the information was updated quarterly. Unlike the bank account hit, which was deemed valid on the spot, job information required an additional verification procedure.

Many jobs showed up as generic companies such as Home Depot, State of New Jersey, or The Sports Authority. In those cases, we entered the information into our database that then automatically searched and provided said company's locations from nearest to farthest from his home. If not in our database, we would call the headquarters and pretext them like I did with Jake the Snake's fugazi delivery on the Toys-R-Us gig. A client's physical employment location was necessary for small and mid-size businesses in New Jersey so that a court officer could serve the wage-execution writ. With the big companies, it didn't matter which location you served as long as it was in the state that the employee worked in. For big companies, the writ always found its way to the legal office in the main office via human resources.

Quarterly job information was not real time, but it had additional strategic value by providing the gross wages a target earned each quarter and that gave us a more complete profile. For example, if the job locate stated for the third quarter of 2010 our target earned $30,456 and he worked for the State of New Jersey Department of Corrections in Trenton, you knew that the target was most likely a corrections officer and he earned around $120,000 annually to stand around and look at guys like me naked. It was guaranteed he would still be there working in that position because it is almost impossible to get fired from a public job. You could locate the exact prison he was stationed at by contacting Trenton and using the FedEx package scam. I know what you are thinking. *Why would a guy who has an excellent state job earning significant coin not pay his bills?* The answer is likely a divorce, girlfriends, kids, drugs, or gambling. Or a combination of all those. Also remember, he probably got that job based on whom he knows, not how much he knows.[77]

So after we processed the list through all banks and job locators, we had already hit a solid 65%. The information was entered into our database of *flukies* and emailed over to our client with a bill that followed on monthly rotation. The billing had three classifications; Banks, Jobs, or Both. Average invoices were between $5,000 and $200,000 depending on the client and the month's hits. Since my clients made twenty times more money than me on the information, they had no problem paying right away. One guy paid me 100 grand in cash that he stuffed in a laser printer box. Not taking many checks had its problems, but they were good problems to have. *Now where did I leave that box?*

The remaining 35% of non-hits were not discarded. They remained in my database and we would periodically re-run them for new bank accounts and jobs. You can run but you can't hide from the collection cheetah. After a year of no action on my exhaustively scrubbed accounts, I finally devised another brilliant scheme to smoke out those motherfuckers from their warm, delinquent caves. This one is going to blow your bloody mind.

I'd promised myself no more risky fronts so as soon as this idea hit me, I swore it would be fast and my last. Even though it may not seem like it, I was acutely aware of the offenses I could be caught doing and charged with, such as mail fraud. Criminal prosecution was always a factor in my decision-making throughout my career. There were many schemes and fronts I thought up over the years and did not implement due to the risk involved. I preferred fronts that didn't require a lot of people. People are the most unstable commodity in the world. Criminals get caught predominately not for what they do, but whom they do it with. They also get caught by whom they do it to. My targets were not innocent figures and my tactics were cloaked. This is why I stayed clear of violence and intimidation as a measure. I knew how effective it was, but I also knew it carried the most heat. (My bust ultimately proved this theory.) At the end of the day, if I saw an angle to exploit in a swift and covert manner, the threat of getting caught never trumped the pursuit of profit. And it never, ever trumped my desire for drugs.

---

77 I'm not worried that I may be pissing off the wrong people and hurting my public sector employment opportunities once paroled. As a felon, I'm not eligible for a state job. Plus, I'm too smart.

So for this new front, I opened a fake corporation called National Rebate Systems, Inc. Once it was properly chartered, I paid a visit to my old drinking buddy, Scott Schroeder, who was the actual president of a bank that only had one single location. He was happy to see me so I gave him one million in cash to be placed in National Rebate Systems' new account at his bank. I asked Scott to order me 100,000 checks that started randomly at #82998 and have the check company add "FOR DEPOSIT BY FIRST PARTY ONLY; NO DOUBLE ENDORSEMENTS ALLOWED" on the back of each one. My buddy was enough of an accomplice already and very handsomely compensated, so he didn't ask any questions.

On to a franchise mailbox store where I opened a new box giving a physical and legitimate address for my new bullshit company. Next stop was Staples, where I purchased 100,000 window envelopes, ten new printers, and dozens of ink cartridges.

Once the new checks arrived, I had my computer comrades come by the very next day. They arrived, already three vodkas deep, at 9am. I instructed them to program the computers to have all the stale debtor names in my database printed onto the checks with each check having the target in the "Payable to" line. Every single check was to be made out in the amount of $10. A letter was also enclosed stating: "Sorry for the delay in processing your refund. We apologize for any inconvenience."

Once my tech commies had the checks, letters, and envelopes printing, I summoned all my employees for a special all-nighter. You know they must have thought they would be taking turns blowing me, but on that night, to their relief (or perhaps dismay), there was actual work to be done. We proceeded to print, stuff, lick, seal, and stamp. Some employers generously buy their employees pizza when they are asked to work overtime. Before we started the night, I placed a huge Waterford crystal bowl in the middle of the table full of cocaine and told everyone to help themselves. Fifteen hours later, the coke was gone and the checks were ready for the mail.

A month later my secretary announced, "Scott is on line two for you."

"What's up, Scotty?"

"Oz, that account you opened last month, your statement is ready and waiting for you."

"On my way."

"Make sure you come in a large vehicle; you're going to need something bigger than your Mercedes."

"Excellent. Gotcha."

I grabbed one of my employees and drove over in his SUV. Inside the bank, I immediately noticed a stack of cardboard boxes. Inside all the boxes were the documents pertaining to my one bank statement. *For one month!* We loaded and left without seeing Scott, who I am sure wanted no part of transporting the contraband off premises.

Back at my desk, I hit the bong[78] and opened the first box to look inside. *Alright, alright, alright! Look at what we have here!* Out of 100,000 checks mailed to our stale debtors, more than 20,000 of these dipshits opened up the envelope and deposited the rebate—my free ten bucks into their very own account. I was ecstatic that all those skivers took my money! Why? Because the check allowed for no double endorsements. Once deposited, the check went to the respective bank's transit department, which posted the $10 to the recipient's account. Then the check was sent to my bank where the payment of the funds was officially cleared by debiting the money from my million-dollar account. At that point, the check ended up in the boxes now sitting on my desk.

All I had to do now was open the box, pull out one check at a time, read the debtor's name off from the front of the check and then flip it over. On the back of the check, I found the bank name and account number which the debtor was kind enough to fill out disclosing exactly the information that my clients were looking for. Remember, these were dead accounts sitting in my computer that I now brought back to life. I copied the check and sent it out to my clients and billed them for the information. I did this 20,000 times over. And many targets that didn't deposit the free money check that month did it the next month. Whenever they did it, *bang! I had them.* And if you didn't cash your free money check, who fucking cares? I kept the ten bucks and lost a stamp.

Once all the boxes were tallied that first month, National Rebate Systems had a score of 20,567 and the debtors had zero. Do the math yourself. My expenses were 100,000 stamped envelopes at 35 cents each, a punchbowl of coke, plus 20,567 times $10 for the checks that cleared. My income was 20,567 hits times 100 bucks per. *Subtract my expenses and I'm going to Disney fucking World!* And like a wise wiseguy, I was in and out of that scam within three months.

---

78 If I haven't mentioned it before, assume I hit the bong every other paragraph.

✦ ◼ ✦

After all the glitter in my life had turned into a steaming pile of dog shit, prosecutors demanded to know, "Did the attorneys who hired you know the information you were selling back to them was obtained illegally?" Even then New Jersey Governor Corzine assigned a task force to answer that question. They were adamant in their belief that my attorney clients must have known I was playing dirty tricks since I was retrieving buried, private, protected information for them so quickly and so cheaply. I know what you're thinking— my prosecutors must have been true master investigators to come to that ingenious conclusion. Nothing short of the largest heist of information in US history that primarily benefited attorneys was in their evidentiary files smacking them repeatedly in the face 1.6 trillion times and these whizzes actually needed to ask me that question to confirm their suspicion. Maybe law school should be one more year. To answer the question to them, I took one out of Uncle Louie's playbook: "I cannot confirm nor deny that allegation." To answer the question to you now—I will most certainly confirm the attorneys simply played dumb. And deaf. And blind. For them this comes natural, because they are the shrewdest, most conniving deaf, dumb, and blind kids on the planet.

But while all that glitters was still glittering in my life, I welcomed any scam that I could profit on. But, I must say, it was hard to keep up with my lawyer clients. Those guys were getting more and more corrupt and greedy by the minute. For someone like me to say something like that would be like someone like me calling someone else a cokehead.

I started seeing some very curious spreadsheets from my attorney clients. On them was data pertaining to recently purchased bad debt from financial institutions. That, in and of itself, wasn't peculiar or the problem. The problem was the attorneys were now unilaterally taking the account balances on the sheet and jacking them up, sometimes as high as 75% from the original balance and importing them into their systems. In the new printout there would be a new, greatly overstated debt balance. Was it legal? Of course not, but it sure as hell worked. The great, immoral legal minds—I know that sounds redundant— that conjured up this fraud figured that since the debtor had been throwing out statements, ignoring letters, and basically denying and hiding for years, they wouldn't know the truth about what they really owed. What about the few who would complain? That is a very rare occurrence in the collection world—when someone calls in angry, actually admits to owing money, but just not as much as you are demanding from them. In those rare circumstances when a debtor did call in to object, the secretaries were using the old, "sorry, it's a typo" defense and would correct it on the spot. Now, I'm no theologian but I think even religious scripture held "False balances are no good!" By my calculation, attorneys were on the highway to hell anyway; this new scam just put them in the express HOV lane. Behind my rocket ship, of course.

One beautiful spring morning, I got call from an attorney client asking if he could hire me for the entire day. I told him I was an amazing and legendary lover but I would not be his gay prostitute. He then gave me the scoop. A group of investors from Texas, known as Texas Star Capital, were going to be in town that day. Texas Star Capital was considering investing five million dollars in New Jersey debt that they would consider placing for collection with the law firm who was now hiring me for the day. The attorney was good at sales but I was Yoda so he preferred I handled the negotiation. Since I knew the debt would eventually end up in my hands for all asset searches, I was definitely interested in prostituting for the day. Truth of the matter was the DRL buzz had officially reached the *country* of Texas[79] and everyone in the industry wanted me somewhere contributing to their bottom line.

I was a high-class hooker so my offer was non-negotiable to the law firm—a fee of $50,000 if I was able to secure the five million dollar investment from the Lone Star cowboys. The attorney reluctantly agreed. He agreed because he was a smart man. Reluctantly—well, because he was a dick, like most of his peers.

I now had only four hours to prepare. The law firm emailed me the contract that I needed to get signed, plus a performance spreadsheet of similar portfolios showing their (meaning *my*) performance statistics for collections for a year. Also included was the Texas trio's flight itinerary as I was to pick up these cowboys at the airport.

Once I printed everything out, I looked at the flight information and saw they were arriving at Caldwell airport, the same private jet airport JFK Jr. departed from the day he crashed and died. When I pulled into the airport with my limo, it was easy to spot my players—three husky, suspender-wearing, half-drunk, skeptical millionaires. If anyone can look like a Yankee-hater from twenty yards away, it was these good ol' boys. They eyed me up and down.

79 That is not a typo; just ask a Texan.

Little did they know that they were staring back at the dirtiest, shrewdest, best-kept secret in the collection industry.

"You fellas must be Texas Star Capital," I said shaking their hands.

"We are sir, we are. This is Buford, this is Earl, and you can call me Big Ed." All three were wide bodies so Big Ed should have really been called Biggest Ed.

"Nice to meet you all.[80] I'm Ozzy."

"Ozzy, my boy—it's been one hell of a flight. Whadda you say we grab a few drinks?" From his breath, I think he should have said a few "more" drinks, but who's counting?

"Okay, fellas you got it. Just a few," I declared while opening my car door for them to get in. My limo fit seven comfortably so it was cramped with us four. We only drove for about three minutes. I decided to go to the Bomber Group, a bar/restaurant located right next to the airport. To be honest, these guys made *me* nervous, which was odd for a guy that is used to being the one making people nervous. In Texas, they give guys like me 50 years just for what I was doing in my bedroom every night, and here I was, supposed to ask them for five million large? This had feds written all over it, so I needed to be step very carefully.

I ordered them a round. Then another. Then another. Then I said *fuck it* and just bought the bottle of whiskey. When that went, I said *fuck it* again and bought a whole barrel. We poured it for ourselves. It kind of felt like we were taking an afternoon saloon break from our cattle run, circa 1895. These Texas longhorns swallowed so much whiskey that it convinced me they weren't FBI. Or, at least they shouldn't be FBI. Federal agents should not be allowed to pound down that hard in a sting operation. Besides I was whiskey-brave by now, so I went for it and whipped out the spreadsheets, performance figures, and started my pitch:

"Gentlemen, New Jersey credit laws are pro-creditor. Unlike Texas, where wage executions are illegal and where you have homestead laws, we do not. Up here, not only do we collect 35% pre-judgment, we also collect another 65% on the post-judgment side. And since we have a friendlier court system, any and all fees are added in to the judgment amount including the constable fee of 10%. So in summary, given that legal landscape, an investment of five million dollars should return 40% plus within the first year. Within the first two years, you should recapture your entire investment plus another ten million.

80 Note that I did not say "y'all".

Thereafter, you still will collect money up to five years out on wage executions and property liens."

These cow-sized boys were stone cold sober and at full attention during the whole pitch. With contract and pen on the table in front of them, I told them not to purchase my services, but rather to invest in them. "What do you think?" I asked.

Big Ed was the first to speak, "Whadda I think? I think that you are one smooth, fast-talking, eye-talian from New Jersey! You need to slow it down, boy!" The others nodded. I looked at my watch and saw what time it was. Time to either lead or follow.

I looked Big Ed directly in his big red face and told him like I was his mother, "Listen—I'm the best at what I do *because* I talk fast, think fast, eat fast, shit fast, and, unfortunately for my girlfriend, I even cum fast. In my business, time is money and if you are slow, you don't collect."

Now it was time to really put them on the spot. I pulled out the one sheet I printed out from my files for the meeting and told them, "Now—either way I will drink with you fine fellas any time, any place, but if want it slow, here is a list of all my competitors. You'll like their speed."

Big Ed smiled, picked up the pen, and signed the contract. "We want results, Mr. Ozzy. Just bring us results."

I poured myself another shot and downed it (and had to fight the vomit back down my throat). I put down the glass down with authority and nodded at him. Big Ed cut the check to the law firm. Then the party really started. Apparently, we were just pre-gaming with the two barrels of booze. Rounds of shots were hoisted and slammed down for the next hour until the pilot called to say he was ready to go. We drove back to the airport and on the tarmac they each hugged me like a long lost brother before they staggered back onto their jet to, no doubt, continue drinking.

Immediately, I called my *pimp* to tell them that I had the contract and his check. "Listen, I'm on my way over to you now," I told him. "Have my check ready for one hundred thousand."

As I hung up on his amateur ass, he was yelling, "The deal was for fifty, not a hundred…!" *Click!* Talk to the dial tone, bitch.

The second he saw my face walking toward his office, he reiterated what he screamed on the phone. "Oz, we agreed on 50,000 if you got the deal, not a hundred—"

I handed him the contract, then the check. It was for ten million, not five. He shook his head and cut my check for one hundred grand. Not bad for my first day as a financial hooker.

The next day, he called me laughing. He was still a dick, though we became pretty good friends. He told me he had spoken with Big Ed a few minutes ago who told him that he loved that fast-talking eye-talian, son-of-a-bitch so much that if he had a sister he would let me fuck her. To me, that was the highest compliment any man from Texas can give, although I did not want to picture fucking Big Edna. Unless she had good teeth.

Texas Star Capital went on to become my all-time favorite client. Every time they came to New Jersey, they let me borrow the company jet for as long as I wanted. *Boy-oh-boy—if that cabin could talk, I would never see the outside of prison again!* I re-invented the term *cockpit* in that corporate plane. The cleaning people probably made thousands just from selling the "dust" from the vacuum bag after my plane parties.

TWENTY

THE TRAGIC EVENTS OF 9/11 FUCKED UP MY MOTOR VEHICLE CONNECTIONS AS THE licenses for the hijackers were issued through the New Jersey Division of Motor Vehicles. It also fucked up my brother Joe irreparably. Joe and I resemble one another and thankfully for him that's where the comparison ends. Joe is a Boy Scout. If he found a penny on the side of the road, he would return it to the police station so the person who lost it could claim it. I, on the other hand, would impersonate that person to claim the penny from the cops. Sure, I resented my honest brother over the years. (It's only natural for schemers like me to harbor a little resentment for those who shoot straight for a living.) But mostly, I despised him because he was always scheming with my old friend Mikey to have me busted for drugs. They never succeeded, by the way.

Joe miraculously survived the attack by being a little late to work that morning. And he was never late. He lost seventy percent of his office that day and fifty percent of his mind. I watched the events unfold on television; not knowing my brother had been late and actually survived until a few excruciating hours later. I kept my face in my snow powder the whole time. It was the only way I knew how to deal with stress—and life in general, for that matter.

Those hours without contact, without knowing and assuming the worst, were the most terrible hours of my mother's life. (And as my mother, she has suffered through some pretty bad ones, before and after.) Joe still hasn't fully recovered, and like so many others, likely never will, from the trauma of watching bodies hitting the ground outside the towers that morning. Some of those bodies were likely his friends.

September 11th made everyone understandably paranoid. As a hardcore drug addict, I was paranoid to begin with. And blindly self-absorbed—so I was worried banking data would become harder for me to breach. I was also concerned about whether my piles of cash, consolidated all in one state, was safe and secure. Eventually, the worry became intolerable for me and I decided to make a dramatic move.

Looking back now, my decision was motivated more by cocaine suspicions than sound reasoning. This was happening more and more. If jet fuel took down all that metal and concrete, I believed my stacks and stacks of highly flammable paper money would not stand a chance.

My plan, on paper, was simple in theory. I would take five million in cash from New Jersey and move it across country to safe deposit boxes in southern California. Why California? Well, I had business to attend to there anyway. But no matter how much planning you do in life, shit happens. Especially when a paranoid, psycho junkie is doing the planning.

My bank contacts in California assisted me in opening the safe deposit boxes under different names. The boxes were held under fake names as primaries and my name as a secondary custodian, giving me unencumbered access at any time. All that was left to do was to physically transport the five million in cash across the continental United States during the height of the terrorist paranoia.[81]

Over the years, I had invested well over a million dollars into my computer systems and every type of high-tech device possible. From pens that were able to record three-hour conversations to military-issued parabolic microphones that enabled you to hear a bear fart in the woods from a thousand yards away, I loved my James Bond toys. They supported all our spying operations (and my

---

81 For obvious reasons, wiring was not an option for piles of off-the-books cash.

sexual fantasies). Now I needed them to use them for personal security reasons.

First, I had to find a travel companion—a female front you could say—to join me on my flight to California. Was it necessary looking back? Of course not, but wait 'til you hear how fun it got. Dina was my first choice. She knew the drill with my business and cash and, more importantly, I figured there was no way she could resist me for three thousand miles in the air. She probably realized that, too, so she turned me down flat, as expected. Next, I turned to Lisa, another well-liked, well-endowed stripper at Dolls.[82] The patrons called her "The Leaning Towers of Lisa" and not because she was Italian. Her height was four foot nothing. Her chest with was four feet wide. Her waist was slimmer than my thigh. When you put it all together in one body, her artificially-enhanced measurements gave her the exoskeleton of a crustacean. And I love seafood!

I invited Lisa to dinner to go over our "vacation" plans, and I immediately realized why they invented Valium. Like me, Lisa was a party girl, and I was totally down with that. But she was also as smart as her jumbo, water-balloon tits required her to be. When the waitress came over, I broke protocol and ordered first, as Lisa was having some trouble reading the menu.

"I'll have the penne with vodka sauce and shrimp," I said. One of my favorites.

The waitress then looked over to Lisa to take her order.

"I'll have the shit-take chicken," Lisa said seriously.

Confused at the order, the waitress leaned over and looked down at her menu to where Lisa was pointing and said while writing, "One she-tak-ee chicken."

Lisa and I looked at each other and both burst out laughing. The waitress couldn't hold back either. I wasn't sure what was worse. The fact that Lisa could not pronounce the word *shitake* or the fact that she was considering eating something with the words "shit" and "chicken" in the name.

The good news after that was I realized I did not have to explain much to Lisa about the reason for our trip. She wouldn't understand anyway. Or care. It was easier to explain to her that we were an engaged couple and we were going on an actual vacation to California. Eventually, (her brain was never in a rush) she came around to realizing I was paying her ten grand cash for two weeks of being my travel companion, decoy girlfriend, and whatever else popped up along the way.

---

82 Where else did you expect me to get a road trip companion, the local church?

The next day, Lisa showed up at my condo wearing a fluorescent pink tight sweatsuit and carrying her most prized possession, Co-Co, her Yorkshire Terrier, who was much smarter than her. We were leaving in a week so I had asked her to stay with me in my condo for our preparation week. We had a lot to prepare for, including getting to know each other in case we had to act like we did. I also had to assess whether or not she was fit for the trip. So far, the only thing I was completely sure of was she was custom built for triathlon sex.[83]

To plot my $5,000,000 cannonball run, I called in a friend of mine who owned a moving company and told him the lie—I was moving my girlfriend to Los Angeles. She, or more specifically her boobies, just got a dancing job out there, so she was moving there ASAP.[84] I explained to him that the entire move was basically one bedroom set and a few miscellaneous items. We scheduled the move for Thanksgiving week and I paid him ten grand in advance. That money was for the move and no questions. I'm certain he was wondering why I would spend ten grand to move one bedroom set so I made it clear the bedroom set was left by her grandmother and had sentimental value to Lisa. I sold it. He bought it. No questions. Done.

The old bedroom set I had stored in my garage would make do. I dialed 1-800-Dial-a-Mattres and left off the last "s" for "stuffing" and ordered a queen-size mattress and box spring to be delivered to my condo the next day. Done.

I called my trusted buddy over at the Passaic County Sheriff's K-9 unit and I asked him to stop by the next day with Zeus, his German Shepherd. I then headed to Home Depot and picked up a few tools along with some mild detergent and color-safe bleach. When I returned, I instructed Lisa to hit the mall to get items that we needed for the trip including some luggage. Before she left, she told me, "Since we are only going to use the luggage for the trip, I'll go to Target and get a cheap set." That was nice of her. She was being frugal. I replied that she could keep the bags when the trip was over.

"Oh, I can keep them?" she said, "Then I'll get them at the Louis Vuitton store—"

"Fine," I replied, smirking. She was dumb, but not that dumb after all. I then told her to stop at a sex shop and purchase some toys and lotions to put inside the suitcases to add to the vacationing couple scam. And just in case of an emergency. Lisa was so gullible that I had her convinced that if you have more

---

83   There should be no need at this point for me to define the three events.
84   Dancing is what strippers say they do to make themselves feel less cheap.

than one dildo, you said *dildi*, not dildos. She was skeptical at first until I gave her an example of the word cactus with the plural cacti. I'm certain to this day she is still mispronouncing the term.

Now for my money plan. We had to wash and dry all the cash. Literally. Why the washing? A contact of mine with the DEA—I told you I had contacts everywhere—advised me a long time ago that all cash that has been in circulation likely has some trace of drug residue on it. He also told me how I could wash the money with to avoid any detection, with color-safe bleach, detergent, and a Downy Ball. This may sound a little crazy but when you were as high as Lisa and I were on coke, the laundry part was a whole lot of fun.

However, when Lisa asked why we had to wash the cash, I told her it was because it was counterfeit and we did not want the ink to run during transportation. Yes, of course, it made zero sense…but did I mention how sensational her mammary pillows were? The bottom line is I didn't want Lisa to think I—hence we—were involved in the transport of so much real money. The reason I framed it as fake money was because that much real money could make any bimbo (or *bimbi*) a clever betrayer. My warning to her was that if she ever told anyone about our little counterfeit run she would never see Co-Co again. She got the message.

Once washed and dried, I re-counted the money (Lisa couldn't help me with that), and then she and I wrapped the five million into bundles with Saran Wrap. Then I unwrapped, counted again, and rewrapped them. Cocaine loves to fuck with you by making you repeat a lot of the things you do. Cocaine loves to fuck with you by making you repeat a lot of the things you do.[85]

I removed a few springs from the mattress and stuffed the cash neatly inside along with a GPS device. Remarkably, Lisa knew had to sew. I told her that her sewing skills, plus being female, were the only two things she had in common with my mother. She did an excellent job repairing the incision and I rewrapped the mattress in its plastic bag. Just like new. It was 5am and I hadn't slept. Cocaine also likes to fuck with you by keeping you up for days.

A few hours later, Zeus arrived with his master. It was funny seeing little Co-Co bark at Zeus when he strutted in. I felt so much safer having this fluffy, three-pound vicious deterrent against any intruders. Zeus ignored Co-Co and went over and sniffed the mattress. No reaction from my expert canine. *Two paws up!*

85 Just fucking with you there—I'm actually clean now.

I crashed for the day. The entire day. Being a cokehead is like being a fireman: you have three days on, one day off. The next morning my mover friend arrived with two helpers. By then, I had GPS devices in every piece. As his Mexican helpers loaded the furniture into the truck, I went outside and gave them both brand new leather bomber jackets for their trip. They were extremely grateful and thanked me at least three times. I replied, "No, *gracias*."[86] When I jokingly told Lisa to do some of the manual labor, she told me sleeping with the movers was not part of our deal.

While the furniture was being loaded, Lisa and I packed her brand new Louis Vuitton suitcases with clothes, lotions, and the famous *dildi*. I also placed GPS devices in our luggage. The movers headed out. Before we left for the airport, I went online and confirmed that all GPS devices were functioning properly. Oh, and I almost forgot one last thing I did—my Colombian pharmaceutical rep stopped by to tape one bag of coke under my ball sac and another in my ass. It wasn't inside my asshole per se; it was just taped in the crack so don't get fucking excited.

Upon arrival at the airport, security was really fucking tight. So were my ass cheeks. There were newly installed metal detectors and there were bomb-sniffing dogs all over the place. There was also a large armed military presence throughout. The Land of the Free and the Home of the Brave was looking more like Beirut. Not a comforting sign when my anal cavity was blocked up with enough contraband to put me away for life. If I farted, the whole airport would have to be evacuated from the white smoke. Lisa and I got scanned and the machine was thankfully unable to detect the bags of coke located in my no-man's land.[87]

During the long flight, Lisa and I got drunk and high by going in and out of the first class bathroom to do lines. Did you ever notice how big those bathrooms are compared to the ones in coach? I did. So did Lisa. That's when it all happened suddenly, even though it had been building up for days. What seemed like a wonderful and wild idea at the time turned into a lifetime of travel delays. Before I knew it, I had Lisa in the bathroom bent over the baby-changing table giving her that *Boom! Boom! Pow!* She was so wet and tight that I forgot we were in the clouds with a crowd of people and started blurting

---

86 Both jackets had GPS devices sewn into them.
87 If you are wondering why I would put everything at risk by transporting coke on my body, just be happy you were never a coke addict.

out loud, "TAKE IT! TAKE IT ALL, YOU DIRTY WHORE!" Or something to that effect.

Surprisingly, there was an immediate knock on the door accompanied by a voice asking, "Is everything all right in there?" I was cumming like a busted fire hydrant, so Lisa, the dirty whore, responded breathlessly, "I'll be done in a minute."

Lisa pulled up her sweatpants (remember the thong stayed on) and exited first. I followed a minute later feebly trying to disguise my post-orgasmic, sweaty, strung-out-on-coke grin. Half the passengers were laughing, the other half were not. Before I completed my walk of shame, one appreciative guy—sitting next to his visibly furious wife of too many years—lipped silently, "Thank you" to me. No—it was my pleasure, really.

A passenger seated in front of us told me that he overheard a stewardess tell another they were making a stop in Las Vegas to "drop these two animals off." Vegas? Damn. If I'd known we were going to Vegas, I'd really have let loose! As the plane was now prematurely descending, I told Lisa to go back into bathroom and get rid of the rest of the cocaine. She told me she had enough. I had to clarify to flush it or they will take Co-Co away forever. She would have jumped out of the plane if I said Co-Co was below us.

One of the curious (or jealous?) stewardesses came over and asked, "Would you like some peanuts?"

I figured I would keep things light so I replied, "No thanks. I already have numb-nuts." She didn't laugh. I was getting a bad feeling.

Fifteen minutes later, we landed on the runway at the Las Vegas airport. Most of the passengers were mad as hell as they now had a delay because of my coke and cock. I looked out the window and waited for the door to open. Suddenly it did.

"Here come the feds," I told Lisa in a low tone.

"What should we do?" she asked.

I took out a magazine and handed one to Lisa. "Play dumb," I whispered.

"What do you mean?" she asked.

"Just pretend you are reading."

Two US Marshals came marching over. One stated in formal tone, "Orazio Lembo, Lisa Kurdock, will you get up and come with us?" *Wow! Talk about customer service. They already knew our names.*

Pretending to be committed to reading, I responded, "No, I'm good."

"Mr. Lembo, I am not *asking* you to get up and come with us; I am *telling* you. Now get up."

I began to talk them out of it—because I'd talked my way out of hundreds of predicaments—but then I remembered the moving truck with five million in cash was en route to California, and America had changed since 9/11. It was time to engage in damage control at this point.

"Come on, honey," I said, grabbing Lisa's hand. "We've been kicked off much nicer planes than this."

This time the entire plane laughed. *Finally!* I worked so hard for that audience. Even the crew and my new federal marshal friends smirked. I could tell that they really didn't want to be doing this, especially after they saw what a sex kitten Lisa was—but everyone had to be more vigilant now. I'd fucked around on planes, blew lines, and fucked girls on planes my whole life without recourse. But from that day on, air travel was never the same for me. Poor Lisa and I were placed on the watch list in the Federal Aviation Administration's "black book" like we were some kind of terrorists. Just for blowing a little blow. And a mile-high load.

Since an airplane was no longer a travel option, we needed to regroup. They gave us our bags after a thorough search and tons of questioning where Lisa certainly acquitted herself better than expected. In the end, they let us go. Luckily, they were men because it must have been, let's say, *interesting* for them investigating the sex paraphernalia and staring at Lisa. In fact, that's likely why they let us go. Kittens are too cute to be left in cages. This is what people mean when they say hot women get all the breaks in life.

I checked in with my truck. It was in Arizona. I called a limousine service, "I need a limo to pick me up and take me to Los Angeles."

"Your name?"

"Michael Hart."

"How long will that be?"

"Should be around twenty minutes."

"Great. One request: please don't send a driver who will kick me out of the car if he catches me having wild sex with a stripper in the back…"

Lisa smiled at me. She was such a kinky little sex kitten. Almost arrested and ready to go again. And I was such a hopeless sex addict.

"Excuse me?" said the dispatcher.

"Oh, nothing. See you in a few."

Twenty minutes later, we were on the road. We were both beat and actually slept all the way to southern California.

The truck met me at my California contact's apartment (I'll call him "Cal") and unloaded the goods. The ride was bumpy, but we made it not a penny poorer. It was time to say goodbye to Lisa with a kiss, five grand more in cash, her new luggage, and a limo ride to her friend's house. Lisa was visibly sad to leave. She had enjoyed the thrill of our adventure and I had enjoyed her shaved, snug pussy, but it was time to break up.

Don't feel sad about our breakup. Later on, we reunited back home for several more happy endings. Who could resist the company of a playful kitten?

My pal Cal was in a business similar to mine and actually still is, which means he hasn't gotten caught robbing and scheming. I was a mentor to him and he was a loyal friend to me. And he will always be a loyal friend to me so that I don't ever get an itch to rat him out and bury him in a prison cell for the rest of his natural life. Anyway, he had already arranged for his contacts at the banks to set me up with enough safe deposit boxes to hold 2.5 million in cash.

The other 2.5 million was used to purchase 125 million in consumer debt originating out of New Jersey that my Cali-connection had arranged. Yes, that is correct, my friends—I was now going into the debt-buying business. Move over big boys, it's time for Ozzy take a seat at the big boy table.

You should be asking yourself, *how did I purchase 125 million dollars' worth of bad debt for 2.5 million?* Hmmmm…let's see…it would be best for me to explain it like this. There's this guy, Steven, who was one of thousands of default debtors that owed on his credit card. Steven's credit card was backed by Washington Mutual, located in California, who naturally wanted to get even with Steven. Now since Steven stopped paying his credit card and ignored all collection letters from them, Washington Mutual charged him off (like I explained earlier) as a loss on their books for that particular quarter. The collection department at Washington Mutual then officially transfers Steven's account to their recovery department. Here's where it gets interesting. The recovery department is set up like a medieval kingdom with one anointed prince. That one guy, and only that one guy, gets to unilaterally decide what to do with all the portfolios of accounts, which are packages of hundreds to thousands of default accounts that are similar to uneven Steven's.

Now the recovery department prince can be—let's say for legal purposes—*directed*. "Directed" as to where he placed those accounts for their recovery. What that means is that the more powerful king of the underground kingdom visits the prince and directs him to either place these accounts at ABC Collection Agency or "sell" them to Asset Recovery Corp, whichever the king prefers. Because the king is the king, and it's great to be the king, his prince always listens. That is how Steven's account inappropriately finds its way onto the desk of the guy writing this story from his bunk in prison.

I was the king in that play. I compensated more than a few princes in recovery departments handsomely, who, in turn, directed the accounts to travel in an agreed upon direction. Thereafter, every time a portfolio was placed for collection and/or sold in my direction, I continued to compensate the handsome prince handsomely. But what had sometimes been known to unfortunately occur is the handsome prince of the recovery kingdom somehow temporarily loses his sense of direction and mistakenly directs a portfolio in the wrong direction. After his loss of directions causes him to nearly fall off the roof of the castle, which most certainly would mangle his handsome face, he usually regains his original sense of direction and everything gets back on course.

◆ ■ ◆

The years 2001 and 2002 were a whirlwind of a ride. I made my biggest returns to date. I lost my brother, then, found him a few hours later. My brother lost his mind. I bought debt. Made bigger and better connections. Everyone felt the impact of terror.

I was getting laid on planes, getting kicked off planes, living like a rock star, fucking like a porn star, washing money literally, washing money figuratively, spending thousands each week on coke for me and my addict posse, and, of course, transporting dildos—I mean dildi.

By the end of 2001, I was the sole owner over $100 million dollars of debt and had become my own client, just like the big boys. For years, I was getting rich locating bank accounts or employment information for customers paying me $100 to $500 per hit. The attorneys and their customers were the ones who always made the lions share off my illegal activities. *Did you hear that, Judge?!* Now let's not forget that it was me and only me who ultimately took the fall for all of us. I'm totally fine with taking all the heat. You can all relax. Enjoy your families, steakhouses, and fancy cars. I'll sit here in this hell in the cell broke, enjoying my shit chili and piss noodles, while you spend the millions I made for you. *You're welcome, fellas!*

Anyway, once I owned all that debt, I could collect it all and make anywhere from $2,000 to $30,000 per hit. I was able to set up much better commission scales for my employees and offer them monthly incentives based on the total dollars they collected for the company.

Best part was I was the guy with the access to all the information. I could have went for it all at that time—first, by cutting off my clients by retiring, and then opening dummy corporations to purchase their book of business when it was deemed uncollectable. It sounded intriguing but that kind of bold move would not have remained a secret forever and would have isolated me as one greedy motherfucker. My philosophy was to always take less and spread the wealth, baby! *Piece and love! Piece and love!*

However, I did take a cue from all the greedy lawyers I dealt with and set up my own "legal model." This front took the attorneys' scam of padding debt even further. By *further*, I meant further away from legality and morality. *I'll take your scam, counselors, and raise you two scams!*

The first part of the scam enabled me to spend ten grand a day on paper, regardless of what I earned in practice. How? I first printed out the raw spreadsheets of data of all the accounts that I now owned. I got a sweetheart deal on the debt because not only was it bad debt, it was very old debt, meaning the statute of limitations on collecting it was set to expire soon.[88] I then put the remaining $2.5 million in my California safe deposit boxes to good and dishonest use. With the help of my Cali-connection, I used my own money and paid my own (debt-owning) company $100 payments on each and every account. Since this new payment was now "the last date of payment" on the debtor's account, the statute of limitations automatically refreshed. *How cool and refreshing!* The consequence: I just bought myself an additional six years to collect on the debt. And yes, since the $100 payment was my cash to begin with it and it went from a bank in California to a bank in New Jersey, it was effectively washed in more ways than one. I got cleaned up and dirtier with the same move.

---

88 The statute of limitations generally starts to run on the date in which the consumer makes their last payment or the month and year when they stopped paying.

Now that the debts were inappropriately freshened-up per the statute of limitations, the second act of the scam was to scrub the accounts squeaky clean. As we were pretending like we were playing by the rules, we sent the debtor the requisite initial demand letter. This written notice was required by federal regulations. Once delivered, you needed to allot the recipient debtor 30 days to "dispute the debt or any portion thereof." *That's it, folks!* Now, since I owned the debt, I was able to rob the debt. What does that mean? Well, it was almost six years (really it was more like six days in the eyes of the law when you factor in my brilliant $100 payment) since the debtor probably looked at his balance. So, I did what every lawyer I serviced was doing and took the face value of the debt, applied a little fuzzy math, until it magically doubled. *So magically delicious!* So now an account that originally had a $3,000 balance (which I bought for 60 bucks) was now a $6,000 debt for collection purposes. *What a lucky charm!*

The initial demand letter served a few purposes. It brought us in "compliance" with federal law, "validated" a new statute of limitations, and "verified" the debtor's home address. If the letter went through and wasn't returned, then the address is considered "verified." If the letter was returned for any reason such as "moved; left no forwarding address" or "addressee not known", then it came back to our office. In the cases that the target chose to forward his mail to his next address, we found out. How? Ever see the phrase in the corner of an envelope by the return address that says, "Do not forward; address correction requested"? Well, that's me. With that statement included on the envelope, the postal service, rather than forwarding your mail to you, returns the letter to me with a cute little yellow sticker that gives me your new address. The United States Postal Service is the most reliable accomplice I ever had. I never got a chance to thank them personally until now. *Thanks boys!*

If the debtor was not smart enough to contact our office and dispute the balance, well, then federal law went from being our biggest pain in the ass to our best friend in the world. If the 30-day dispute period expired without a response from the debtor, the debt, along with the newly-inflated balance, was now deemed valid. If the debtor did contact us, we would sell them on how the credit card companies rape consumers with interest and then we would sell them on a 50% settlement. That 50% settlement amounted to a ninety-plus percent profit to us. Funny how subjective math can be.

Obviously, any debtor smart enough to call in response to the demand letter was handled very delicately. This was a code red matter, the equivalent of grenade without the pin in it. We did not want the banking commission investigating our records and seeing our fuzzy mathematical formula.[89] So I was very accommodating to those debtors in cutting them deals.

Once I know the address is good and you did not dispute the debt, it is then ready for suit. Lawsuits were always my last resort and I made them the final front. I promise you (again) this is the last front. When you filed a civil suit against an individual in New Jersey on behalf of a corporation, it needed to be filed by a licensed attorney. Since I don't like or trust attorneys—no, I take that back, I do trust attorneys. I trust that they will fuck you and me every chance they get. So why pay a scumbag—I mean, an attorney for something I could do myself? They weren't interpreting offshore tax shelter laws here—they were filling out the same simple paperwork over and over again. And billing me out the ass for it like it was a capital fucking murder case.

Instead of hiring an attorney, I did one step better and bought one. I bet you didn't even know they were for sale. *Everyone is for sale, my friends!* My pet attorney's name was Mario Mindurbusiness. I got him his own office decked out with legal books, an Xbox, and a Gameboy. Super Mario sat at his desk and played *Super Mario* all day while we used his license hanging on the wall directly over his head to do our lawyering. With all the proper legal formalities out of the way, the only chance a debtor had against me was to either file for bankruptcy (which they usually did long before the account got that old) or move to another state or country and hide. Hide and seek was my favorite game to play.

I took great pleasure in abusing the court system to enforce my rights as a litigant against debtors. The courts made me a court-ordered creditor. *What an honor, Your Honor!* You may have opened the credit card originally with Chase Bank, but the court just deputized me to chase your ass all the way down to Chinatown for the money.

As a "licensed attorney" in the State of New Jersey, I bundled all my summonses and complaints together, added in my improper legal fees, and sat back with my bong as the court handled the rest. The court served the defendant and gave them 30 days to file an answer. I already had proof that the address

---

89 Actually, we did not want any regulators knowing we even existed.

was good, so statistically 95% of my cases resulted in a default judgment. That meant only 5 out of 100 lawsuits I filed were actually contested by the debtors. For the other 95, the summons probably went in the garbage, the same place all the previous bills and collection letters did for the last several years. Once the 30 days was up, I was awarded the default in writing, which was used to levy bank accounts. You already know I was an expert at locating those bank accounts through my system of bribes and false pretenses.

One might be inclined to wonder about what happens to the 5% who actually answer the summons. If you were a merely practical and not fanatical human being, you might say the hell with the dead 5%. After all, with an astounding 95% winning percentage in court on inflated numbers no less, you could easily forget about the remaining 5% and not be hassled. But I was the master of hassle and a master hustler. I never turned away from a penny I could steal.

The rare debtor that answered a summons needed to state in writing the grounds for not owing the money. It was always a different answer, depending on the circumstances, so I dealt with them on a case-by-case basis. For example, if the debtor answered by requesting "proof of the debt" (which by law they are entitled to) I did what I do when I wake up to a hideous girl in bed next to me asking for my phone number. I make one up. My computer system was Russian-built, which meant it was filled with the corporate letterhead of any company you could ever have possibly owed money to in the world. I had everyone's logo, including Disney's. A little cut and paste and *poof!* I had an authentic-looking statement from a corporation with a click of the (Mickey) mouse. *That is the real magic of Disney, folks!*

My "poof" proof of the debt was sent into the court. Since I'm an officer of the court (or pretend to be), my word and oath are attached to this whole scam—I mean evidence—and the debt is considered valid.

Some guys actually still went to court (or threatened to) in order to battle it out in front of Judge Idontgiveashit. In those rare circumstances when I got notice from the court to show up for the hearing because Mr. Deadbeat still claimed "he doesn't owe this money" instead of interrupting my real lawyer in the middle of his Super Mario game, I program my Caller ID Jammer to register the appropriate county court information and play a little game of my own with Mr. Deadbeat:

Ring!

"Hello?"

"May I speak to Mr. Craig Gia, please?" I'm courting him using my court voice.

"This is Craig Gia." *Nice, our defiant debtor is on the line.*

"Mr. Gia, this is Michael Hart with the Bergen County Court, Special Civil Division."

"How may I help you?"

"I'm calling in reference to an answer you filed with court on docket number SC-09769-02. This is the matter scheduled for trial on August the 9th."

"Okay."

"Well, it appears that the attorney for DRL Associates has faxed us a notice to dismiss the complaint against you."

"Really, they did?"

"Yes sir. I received it yesterday, and the case has been removed from the calendar."

"That's great. Do you know *why* they dismissed it?"

"Who knows? Maybe they saw your answer and figured they didn't want to mess with this guy."[90]

"Wow! Okay—so what happens now?"

"Nothing. Since they dismissed it, it's over. That's why I am calling you. You win."

"So I don't have to come to court on August 9th?"

"If you want to, you certainly can. And park your car four blocks away, go through three metal detectors, then wait three hours in the courtroom to hear your case being officially dismissed by the judge on the record due to withdrawal of plaintiff's complaint."

"Oh yeah. I'm familiar with that," says our deadbeat. "That's all you do when you go to court—sit and wait. Five years ago, I waited in court for six hours for a $50 parking ticket. I missed an entire day of work."

"Well, now you don't have to, if you don't want to. Like I said—you'll receive written confirmation to your home address of 2451 Bath Avenue in Bogota after the formal dismissal on August 9th."

"Okay, great! Thank you for calling and letting me know."

---

90 That actually sometimes happens, just not in this case.

"You're welcome, Mr. Gia. Have a good day, sir."

"Take care." *...of my money that I'll soon be levying from your bank account.*

At this point not only does this asshole think he's a great litigator, he believes the case is dismissed and decides not to show up to court on the court date. *Big fucking mistake, counselor!* The result for me is another default judgment. By the time Mr. Deadbeat realizes what hit him, I already hit his bank account and buried him in paperwork. *Litigate that, bitch!*

The lesson here is the same as when Adrian yelled to Rocky when he wanted to fight that big Russian steroid monster, "YOU CAN'T WIN!" If you could win, I wouldn't have had bricks of coke in my house and millions in cash hidden all over the country.

When it came to dealing with me or my cronies, either way you were fucked. I hunted you down like a wolf chases prey and if I couldn't find you, I went after your family. And if you didn't have family, I went after your dog. And if you didn't have a dog, I waited. A judgment in the State of New Jersey was good for 20 fucking years. Sooner or later, I got you. *Fuck you, pay me!*

Post-judgment, you were locked in my radar and had very little hope to avoid me. In one swoop, I pulled your credit report illegally and reported the debt you owed us to the credit reporting agencies, where it would stay until the six-year statute of limitations was over. My cock was blocking any financial move you ever tried to make from that point on. My alternative offensive was entrapping you to contact us with our UPS fake *Sorry we missed you* labels, which should have said "Sorry, I'm here to fuck you right through the pants." After my target debtor called in and was told the "wrong house", we waited fourteen days before calling them back, to create safe distance between the two events. The call back was my classic reverse collection script. If it was a bad check, I would contact the debtor as a sheriff's deputy, poised to arrest the debtor. Debtors were always very respectful and willing to do anything you asked to avoid getting their tight asses raped in jail.

My team used these same cruel and unusual tactics. They were calling debtors as sheriff's deputies ready to serve a civil summons but they would give debtors a chance to contact Michael Hart and see if they could resolve the matter first.

Remember we were pretexting debtors, but *not* financial institutions, which

HR 4943 outlawed. Both Presidents Clinton and Bush would have been so proud!

✦ ■ ✦

I was bothered by the fact that certain debtors were still on my list of uncollected debt, so I decided to create my final front. *This is the last one, I double-dog swear.* Finding assets was enjoyable detective work, but also an expensive proposition. I was paying bribes to insiders and commissions to my people for basically every bit of information. Like all businesses, labor costs were the most expensive expenditure. Don't get me wrong—I was generous to people for a reason, as my team definitely deserved it. However, if I could somehow find a way to lessen labor costs on my personally owned debt, my returns would skyrocket. One day, when I opened the mail, it hit me like a fat tit in the face during a lap dance. *Delaware! All credit card offers originate from Delaware!* Like George Washington, it was time to take a boat and cross over to Delaware! Or was it Pennsylvania?[91] Either way, this was just as monumental.

First, I did what any horny guy does first: dialed one of my best booty-girls, Marissa, and told her to clear her schedule. We were taking a road trip to Wilmington, Delaware, for a few days of sex, drugs, and criminal mischief. Once my "travel ass" was reserved, I paid a visit to an old friend from my Uncle Louie days, Lenny the License. I hope his name is self-explanatory. He didn't have a phone, so you could only see him in person, just like medieval times again.

Knock. Knock.

"Who is it?!" an unfriendly voice snapped. Imagine this guy's mood on Halloween.

"It's Ozzy."

After seven dead bolts were unlocked, the door opened. "Holy shit! Fucking Ozzy Lembo, where the fuck have you been?"

"I've been doing my thing, Lenny."

"I heard you went legit?" Only a wiseguy would call what I was doing legit.

"Yes, over ten years now." *A decade of decadence.*

"It's great to see you. What brings you by?"

"I need a haircut."

"I don't do haircuts," he said. Then he came over to me and patted me down like he was Secret Service. Maybe he was concerned I was wired, or he was a

91 As you can imagine, I was high during most of my history classes.

closet gay groper, or he was a physician. Whatever he was, I thought he should have at least asked me to cough when he squeezed my ball sac.

"Prices are way up since 9/11," he told me.

"Really?" I said. Honestly, I was just happy the sexual assault was over.

"Yeah, with the hijackers having New Jersey haircuts and all, it scared away a lot of people."

"So, how much are we talking?"

"Five K."

"For one fucking haircut?"

"Yes, sir."

"What if I wanted a Delaware cut?"

"Then it's 2K."

With that, I handed him the required small picture of myself. "Here's what I want it to look like."

"What name should I put in the appointment book?" he asked.

"Paul Stewart."

"Okay. Your appointment is for Wednesday at 1pm. If you're one minute late, it gets canceled. No refunds."

Handing him two grand in cash, I pointed out "Those are pretty harsh rules for an old friend." And after that pat down, we were technically lovers, really.

"Who said we're friends?" he replied and shut the door.

You have a good day, too, I said under my breath and walked away.

Next, it was on to see Lei, a friend of mine, a graphic designer from somewhere in Asia where girls are really sexy. She had designed projects for me in the past as she worked for a huge advertising company in New York City and did side jobs from her home. I love women who moonlight.

Lei and I actually never met face to face until the day I went to her apartment to discuss my new project in private. I got understandably sidetracked during this process.

Ding! Dong! (obviously, I'm ringing the doorbell, you filthy-minded dog.)

There she was. Slender. Older. Sweaty. Barely covered with a sports bra that couldn't contain her protruding nipples and matching spandex workout shorts that revealed no panties.

"Lei?" I asked looking straight at her nipples instead of her eyes. *How hot,* I thought to myself, *her name is pronounced "Lay"*.

"Oz-zee?" she replied in her adorable Asian accent.

Wow, all of the sudden I was in the mood for Chinese food. Or Korean. Or Japanese. Or Vietnamese. I wasn't really sure. Although Lei never met me in the flesh, she knew what I was all about from our phone conversations. She gave me the *I-know-what-you-want* smile while I stood there and undressed the rest of her in my head.

"You're stunning," I confessed.

"Oh—thank you, you're very sweet."

"No, I mean it. You are one hot tamale. Or, I mean, hot dumpling." I didn't know what to say I was so turned on.

"Did you come here to compliment me?"

"No, but I didn't plan on my erection, either."

"You're cute," she said smiling. "But you're too young for me."

"Did you say too hung? Or too young?"

"Young!"

"Sorry, I couldn't tell with the accent." With that, I handed her an envelope and took an imaginary cold shower in my head.

"I need 20,000 of those applications made out to everyone on the enclosed list," I told her as she reviewed it. "I will email you the return address in a couple of days to put on the application. Then, call me when it's ready. Or before, if you're ready to start having meaningless, glorious sex."

"Goodbye, Oz-zze!"

It was worth one last try. "Listen, Lei. I'm going to have sex with you tonight whether you're there or not. You might as well come and enjoy it."

Slam.

Ouch! She shut the door on my hopes and wet dreams.

On Wednesday at 1pm—exactly at 1pm, I got my haircut from Lenny. Paul Stewart's hair was cut perfectly.

Then I swung by and picked up Marissa, who was wearing her hair pulled back, with skin-tight hot pants that hid not one inch of her curvaceous figure. Marissa was no stripper but she was definitely a fast machine who kept her motor clean. And she was one of the best damn women that I've ever seen. The fact she was a grammar school teacher turned me on. The fact that she was a conservative church girl turned me on. The fact that every curve on her was real turned me on. Stepping into my Mercedes, Marissa wore a huge red smile and emitted sex instantly with her perfume. She knew I was not merely a man, I was an adventure. And she was a sexual thrill seeker, too, so it wasn't long before I was getting road head.

We drove down to Cape May and checked into Congress Hall, a conservative, upscale hotel right on the beach that was not at all accustomed to the cocaine-abusing, sex fanatic demographic. Marissa loved sugary alcohol drinks but not with cocaine…so I was forced to do double to make up for her slacking. What I liked most about Marissa is she looked and acted like a calm, conservative good girl but behind closed doors, she was a total sex savage. She was not one to whisper "I want you to make love to me, dear." *Make love to me?* I wouldn't know how. She would smack me in the face and growl in my ear, "Fuck my ass! Now!" She was so into the sex that night, I had her fuck Paul Stewart, too. By the time we woke up the next morning, the headboard was broken and the guests next door were exhausted from a sleepless night.

After we ate breakfast with cold stares from fellow guests, we jumped on the Cape May-Lewes Ferry.[92] You actually drive your car onto the ferry and in one hour, you drive off and you're now in Lewes, Delaware. Once there, we started our drive to Wilmington, and that's when the Q&A started.

"Orazio?" Now I knew it was serious as I was being addressed formally by a teacher.

"Yeeees?"

"Where are we going?"

"I told you already. Wilmington."

"And where in Wilmington are we going?"

"The post office."

"We drove all the way here *just* to go to a post office?"

"No. We drove here to have anal sex and *then* go to the post office."

Now I could tell she was really curious. "I may have smacked you too hard in the head last night," she said, "but did you forget there are post offices in New Jersey?"

"Yes, I'm well aware of that. And no, you didn't smack me too hard last night, but you can certainly try again tonight, you little vixen, you!"

"Oh—you're in big trouble tonight!"

"I can't wait."

---

92 I told you I was traveling like George Washington.

We pulled up to the post office. "Now, why are we at this post office?"

"Marissa, there is this federal offense called accessory before the fact. Wait here and think about what that means and whether you want to continue this conversation when I get back."

Once inside, Paul Stewart paid for the biggest postal mailbox they had and called in the box number to Lei.

A few days later, the bogus applications from the bogus company called Future Credit Card were completed and printed off by Lei. They looked great and became an unequivocal financial scam success. The motto was "Your future is now!" but should have been "Your future is fucked!" All the respective recipients (who happened to owe me on debt I owned) were guaranteed a $10,000 unsecured credit card, as long as they had one of the following: a current verifiable job or bank account. All you had to do was return the application meeting those criteria and you were guaranteed approval. I knew consumers always looked at the fine print for a catch, so I included one. It read: *if you have only a verified job or an open bank account, your credit line will be $5,000 and if you have both a verified job and an open bank account, your credit limit will be $10,000.* I also made it time sensitive, stating all applications must be received back in no later than 30 days.

Out of 20,000 credit card applications mailed out, I received back approximately 4,100 responses. It cost me a little more than $25,000 for the applications, mailing, license, and other miscellaneous items, but it ended up bringing in over $5,000,000 in levies and seizures. *Not a bad investment, if I say so myself!*

The only catch was it was a one-off front. I knew the Wilmington Post Office in Delaware would get hammered with calls screaming about the Future Credit Card company right around the time my debtors received a notice of bank levy or wage execution. Unfortunately, this meant Paul Stewart had to disappear. Too bad... he was so young and had great hair.

TWENTY ONE

L ATE ONE DAY, DINA CALLED AND SHE TOLD ME SHE MIGHT HAVE HOOKED A WHALE. A *dancer friend*[93] of hers from Long Island had a *special customer*, meaning a sugar daddy, who worked at the IRS, or as I preferred to call it the "Mecca of Information." This guy was allegedly a family man and reputable professional when the lights were on, but a raging alcoholic and sex fiend when the lights went off. *My kind of guy!* The best news of all was he was scheduled to retire right after tax season the next year. So the plot thickens.

Strippers—I'm sorry—*dancers* typically rotated around different clubs in a wide geographic region. This provided male customers with an influx of new faces, titties, and asses while providing the entertainers a large customer base. This is how strippers in New Jersey knew all the strippers from Long Island, Connecticut, and even Florida. Now don't go around telling people that I said all strippers were hookers. They were certainly not, but many had sugar daddies, like me. So don't go around telling people I was not a great father, either. I supported all my kids. What other daddy do you know who paid for dozens of fake boobs?

93 Again, this means someone who grinds on you naked for money.

Right off the bat, I respected this intriguing IRS guy for at least paying to get laid, rather than paying to imagine getting laid. That is what porn is for. We went over that already. Guys who frequent strip clubs and don't get laid really irk me. Why wouldn't you simply go on Craigslist, get a hooker, a hotel room, and an eight ball? With that setup, you would at least return to home satisfied. Why sit on a barstool all night, throw money away, and leave a few hours later broke and, even worse, with a raging hard-on? It makes no sense physically. Or financially. I'm no doctor, but I know enough about the male anatomy to know *still* semen, like still pond water, is poisonous to men and must be drained from your balls at least daily or you can die from it.

Seriously, I believe this type of paying-to-gawk behavior actually compounds sexual frustration, which can be a breeding ground for sexual and other violent crimes. Men who pack in sexual frustration like a Civil War cannon without proper release are a danger to society. That is one of the many reasons why I am a strong advocate for legalizing prostitution. And allowing prostitutes to have conjugal visits with prisoners. At least those locked up in New Jersey.

Anyway, Dina arranged an appointment for the following week for me to meet Fred the Fed.[94] The idea was for me to drive out to a Long Island bar and see if I could persuade Fred to work for me. He was a guy so it was purely about whether he wanted to earn extra cash for his retirement. In my assessment, Fred was already sufficiently criminalized by paying Dina's friend for sex, so I was pretty sure this was no sting operation or some kind of setup. It goes without saying that I was very excited for this once-in-a-criminal-lifetime opportunity. I feel like doing a line of coke just reminiscing about it, except I'm in jail.

As you know my information contacts were deep and unprecedented, but they were predominately local. If I caught an IRS insider whale in my net, I could fish targets nationwide and be bigger than US Steel!

Walking into the bar, it was dark and crowded for happy hour. A quick scan and I saw Fred over on a stool dressed in a suit that he must have been wearing for all of the 24 years he served unhappily as an IRS agent. Just by looking at his face, I could see into Fred's boozing wild side. It is customary for dogs to sniff each other's asses to see where a stranger has been and what a stranger is all about. However, human dogs, like me, can detect moral decay just by

94 Obviously not his real name, but you and the feds don't ever need to know his real name.

looking into a stranger's eyes.[95] Fred's eyes were all I needed to gaze into. The eyes, they say, are the windows to the person's soul. And Fred's windows were clearly shattered.

Fred was divorcing, which meant going broke. Dina said his only vices were women and booze. Too bad he didn't do coke, but I assumed he was subject to random testing at his job. He certainly looked like a willing partaker if he could. No problem, more coke for me.

After pleasantries, Fred got right down to Chinatown. "My friend tells me you wanted to speak to me about business."

"Indeed, I do."

"She also told me you were a serious businessman. Is that correct?"

"I'm very serious," I replied.

He was feeling me out. Fred didn't know me from Oprah Winfrey so it was not unreasonable for him to suspect I was there to set *him* up. I've been in his shoes my whole adult life, so I knew exactly how to ease his concerns. Before he could ask, I jumped his next question, "Follow me—I want to show you something before we talk any further."

Fred put down his drink and followed behind me outside and over to my limo where my trusty driver immediately opened the door for us. I allowed Fred to get in first. As soon as I was inside, I locked the door and started undressing. I took it all off like a clumsy, gay stripper. Fred was visibly uneasy. He must have been wondering if I wanted to fuck him or I forgot to take my meds.

"What the hell are you doing?" he demanded to know.

I didn't answer until I was done undressing and Fred had a front and center row seat for my full frontal nudity show.

"I'm showing you how serious I am," I told him matter-of-factly.

"Okay, okay! I get it. Now please get dressed." He was not looking at me, which I admit I was a little insulted by.

As I dressed back up, I explained how I wanted someone to provide me with current employment information on a national level. I would provide the names and socials needed to pinpoint the target's employment location. Fred listened carefully then spoke, "I have the access and authority to deliver what you need but sorry, I don't have the interest."

Oh, I see…we're playing chess, not checkers. I looked at my watch and saw <u>what time it was. *Time for* checkmate!</u> At that, I opened the ice bucket and took

95 Although, come to think of it, I'm pretty sure an ass whiff would reveal a lot, too.

out twenty grand in cash and dropped it on the seat. I told him, "Maybe we can start very small and if you're comfortable—and only if you're comfortable—over time, you may get more and more interested."

Fred looked at me, clearly contemplating the gravity of the situation, which probably meant he was imagining how much more fun retirement would be wearing a President Rolex and banging twin island babes in the Dominican Republic.

I didn't follow up. Instead, I opened the door to let him out. He didn't take the cash. Another wise move. Before I closed the door, I ended my pitch with, "I need a month's advance notice if you want to run a test. I will need that time to accumulate all the questions."

"What's a test worth?" he turns around and asked.

Ahhhh—finally! We're talking numbers. "The test is about 1,000 questions long to start and worth 250 points for every correct answer…" I gave him one last moment to do the math on how much island pussy that cash buys. "…and this is the last time we will ever meet. Business will flow through your trusted friend from now on."

I closed the door and pulled away.

A week later, Dina brought me best news of my life.[96] My friend Fred was interested in taking the test, once and only once. I immediately went into my wall safe and pulled out twenty grand in cash, handed it to Dina and told her how bright the future was. And it was at that moment. But there were very dark clouds threatening to ruin everything.

However, this was not the time to worry about the tsunami of legal problems just over my horizon. I've been asked whether I knew it was coming. Yes and no. *Yes*—during the rare times I was sober and honestly examined my life. *No*—all other times.

Having a blockbuster insider waiting in the wings to expand my criminal aspirations ironically gave me positive motivation to commit to getting clean. In Ozzy logic that meant drink, smoke weed, and fuck whores, but try not to do coke anymore. The coke was really the dark cloud in my gathering storm. My life was running too fast already. Fueled by cocaine, it was speeding away from my control. There was too much for me to gain from not being a slave anymore to the almighty powder. I had to try and break free. The good news is I had done

96 No—she still didn't want to fuck me, but be patient. It gets better. And worse.

it before. My record up until that date was a little over eight hours. I was sure I could beat that.

I needed to get back to California to begin my takeover of the world. These next few months would prove to be the most critical of my life. I was intent on making all the right connections and deals with my peers across the country before I put Fred the Fed to the test. Most tellingly, I was traveling without cocaine for the very first time since my parents used to take my brother and me down to the Jersey shore.

Upon arrival, my first meeting was with Cal to fill him in on my (and thus *his*) new business opportunity. Well, technically my first meeting was at my hotel, the Beverly Wilshire in downtown Beverly Hills, to fill in my favorite California girl, Lily. Lily and I engaged in our customary spanking, biting, and filthy talk, but what made it most memorable for me was that it was a coke-free engagement. I had not fucked anyone, including myself, without the influence of coke in probably over a decade.

There are so many more women I could write about in my story. I'm not bragging—believe me, most of them were not the kind of women you write about. But Lily was different. She was a rare breed of woman in my crazy life, blonde with brains. I was used to bimbo strippers and illiterate models, most of whom I wished turned into a pizza 30 seconds after we had sex. Some were street smart but almost none were book smart like Lily. And book smart, I discovered, turned me on. Admittedly, I was easily turned on but I was particularly attracted to Lily's brains. She was college-educated and she owned an art gallery, which made for great role-playing and, believe it or not, great after-sex conversation. Lily made everyone around her happy with her quick wit and bubbly personality. She also made every male around her horny with her perfectly toned bubble butt. Her body was a wonderland, meaning everyone, including John Mayer, wondered what it would take to get in her panties. I loved that.

Eventually, despite my fierce emotional resistance, I even started to like Lily. Relax—I didn't say love, I said like. But what I did love was southern California. It fit my personality and it definitely loved me back. If there ever was a lifetime achievement award given out for criminal impersonation, the Oscar would go to Ozzy. Further, thanks to the popularity of *The Sopranos*, Californians loved Italian guys from New Jersey as much as their wine and burritos.

All right. Enough with the sappiness. It was time for business. I left Lily at the spa and headed over to Cal's office. The second I walked inside, I spotted his assistant Gary with his bloodshot-eyes and right thumb up in the air. I knew what time it was.

Gary was one of those geek students who got straight As in science class and then used his skills to attain "high" places. Half-chemist, half-horticulturist, and all stoner, Gary grew acres of the best pot I ever smoked in my life. That review, mind you, is coming from a renowned druggie with a long resume. Since I was abstaining from the white powder, I needed pot more than oxygen. Truth is, marijuana, although classified a drug, is really medicine for people like me. Or a vitamin.

And truth be told, there is no doubt in my mind that if I had stuck to just smoking weed and not doing coke, I wouldn't be in prison right now. And I wouldn't have made as much money. On the bright side, a drug counselor once told me that if I had started drugging fifteen years later, I would have been dead from crystal meth. Timing is so important in life.

I walked over and bro-hugged Gary. As soon as he opened the top drawer, a potent scent rolled out and punched me in the face like Mike Tyson.

"What the fuck is that?" I asked.

"Purple haze, my man, purple haze." I love stoners. Especially California ones where they originated. Great dudes. Non-violent. Happy. Always snacking. Always in the same clothes. I would have been considered a stoner, except I did rocket fuel drugs, on top of all the weed.

I grabbed the bag, dropped $500 in its place, and shut the drawer, which to me was a great deal. I thanked Gary and strutted into Cal's office, where Cal greeted me with another bro-hug. Weed is so social.

Cal then looked at me funny and then said, "You look *different*."

"Fuck you," I answered uncomfortably.

"No shit, dude," he replied seriously. "You really look different...in a good way."

What he really meant, but didn't realize, was that he never saw me not high. Some people had a poker face. I had a coker face.

We started talking shop. I told him how we knocked it out of the park with the debt purchase he previously arranged for me. It was the first time in DRL history, I explained, the collection numbers were greater than the asset numbers.

He was floored. This set the table for my next point.

"What if I told you I came here because I have a better opportunity than that one for you?"

"Are you fucking serious?"

"You bet your fucking balls I am. I'm 100% sober for the first time since puberty. You do the math."

"Talk to me…"

"The information I access in New Jersey is now accessible in California and every other state in the whole United fucking States, including fucking Guam. If you give me a name and social security number, I'll get you a hit!"

"What's the rub?" *There's always a rub, isn't there?*

"There are two. First, it's $500 per hit. Second, it's a one-off."

Hours of discussions later resulted in our decision to purchase as much big balance debt in California as possible, add in $500 for Fred's fee and the *administrative costs*[97] from DRL to the balances along with other bogus miscellaneous fees and then run them all. That was the plan with Cal and me. I also had a plan of my own, without Cal.

At 500 a shot, I already decided to solicit every prominent collection attorney in the country that was looking for job locates on their target debtors. I labeled the project Operation Nationwide and General Ozzy was planning on hitting every convention, workshop, and seminar for the next few months to put together a huge list for my one-time, once-in-a-lifetime score. This was my Lufthansa heist.

As I walked out of Cal's office after bro-hugging goodbye, his secretary told me I looked different. *Enough is enough!* I blurted back to her the difference was that I was sober.

A few days secretly without cocaine and the whole world took notice. Later when I called my mother, she immediately told me I "sounded better." Then she started in again.

"When-a you-a getting-a married?" she asked.

"May," I said.

"May-a!" she replied in shock.

"Yeah, Mom," I announced. "May the day never come!"

My mother probably knew she caught me while I was sober for the first <u>time since high school. I</u> would imagine most adult children prefer to talk to

97 You know, the cost of bribes, blow, boobs, and blowjobs.

their parents under some form of medication or intoxication. My mother seized the clear moment and started telling me about how I can't live my life partying. How I can't just chase girls and chase money. How without a family of my own I was going to regret my life. I paid little attention and let her get it all out. However, I couldn't take any more when I heard her tell me all my money will never buy happiness.

"Did you see my new Mercedes yet?" I asked and hung up.

I really needed to get high.

Back at the hotel, Lily smoked a jumbo-jet joint with me. *Talk about magnificent weed! Mother Nature can sure fuck you up! Bravo!* Clueless and so happy about it, Lily and I ended up completely lost in downtown Beverly Hills for an hour. Funny thing was Lily grew up there and was more lost than me. Did I mention how splendid Gary's weed was? I think I am still high from it writing this sentence.

Anyway, we finally found our way back to the hotel, still as glassy-eyed and giggly as when we left. We got into the elevator and it was hilarious. No reason. Everything is hilarious when you're that stoned. Before the elevator door closed four, seven-foot tall black guys got in with us. That was funny also, even sober. They looked at how stoned we were—it was impossible to disguise—and then they looked at each other and laughed, which made us laugh more. Still laughing, they got off on our floor and one guy bent down to ask me "Hey man, can I score me some fun?" *That's all your main man Ozzy, Master of Ceremonies, needs to hear...*

"My man! Of course, come on in," I said smiling. Three of the four walked in our room. And the fourth guy went to go get a fifth guy. Now there were 35 feet of men in my room.

Flame on! Party on! And just like that, we were partying with the Minnesota fucking Timberwolves. We smoked a few fatties and laughed nonstop for about an hour. Then—ready for this—one of the dudes looks at his watch and yells, "We gotta go!"

While we hugged goodbye, I asked, "What's the rush?" Joints make people best friends for life in five minutes, so goodbyes are difficult.

"We got a game," one uttered as they hurried out.

A game! Was he talking about a game? Not practice! A game! Holy shit, Batman—these guys are taking on the mighty Lakers in a little while completely baked on Gary's finest herb.

I was on my cell dialing my bookie connection back home before the door shut. He checked the line. The Lakers were favored by eight. I told him to put me down for 100 grand on the Lakers minus the eight.

In stereo, both my bookie friend and Lily screamed out, "A HUNDRED THOUSAND!"

"Yes, a hundred fucking thousand! But DO NOT place the bet in any of Uncle Louie's offices, understand?"

"I got you, Oz. You ain't no big gambler so you must—"

I cut him off. "You can bet it, too. Just you," I said and hung up.

The Lakers won only by twelve. They must have been stoned, too.

With a few days "sober", I had more luck flowing than the past few years inhaling an entire tropical forest of the coca plant. To be fair, Purple Haze, booze, and Lily's luscious ass kept the vicious physical edge off, but I was definitely itchy for my super powder. I spent the rest of the week relaxing and shopping with Lily while plotting to storm the industry with my nationwide strategy. Lily was still a blast to be around. She was sensitive and smart for Big Ozzy. And an amazing temptress for Little Ozzy. She loved modeling bathing suits for me at swanky boutiques until I couldn't take anymore and raided her dressing room with Little Ozzy in tow.

Lily, I could tell, was thoroughly enjoying the soberer Ozzy, and truth be told, so was I. She kept telling me how proud of me she was. At the end of our week of relaxation and romance—okay. There. I admitted it; it was romantic—she leaned over and whispered in my ear the scariest words I ever heard in my life, "I love you."

It felt like a sniper had shot me. *How fucking disrespectful to blindside me with that!* I responded as any male ought to, "Please don't say that."

"I'm sorry, but I do," she replied. Her tone indicated she was almost as upset about it as I was.

What the fuck is going on? I couldn't believe I had to deal with this. All I wanted was head and got a headache instead. I wasn't ready to deal with that word or that feeling. I was only in my early 30s, not in my late 80s, when men like me might consider settling down. Her words were a blatant act of emotional terrorism. Unforgivable.

Little Ozzy and I knew at that exact moment that the best way to make Lily happy was to leave her. And so I did. I flew back to the east coast the next day. I told Lily that I'd be back in California very soon. It was a true statement... except that I never returned to her.

When I arrived back at my New Jersey office, my bookie buddy was waiting for me as instructed. He waltzed into my office shaking his head and dropped a stuffed manila envelope on my desk. "How the fuck were you so sure?" he asked.

"Purple haze, brother, purple haze."

The next major collection agency convention was in California in another week. It was time for Ozzy to blow up the country. Everyone who was anyone in the collection industry would be attending. The objective was if they didn't know me yet, they soon would. My reputation was already nationwide from the huge numbers and volume I was handling in New Jersey. If they ever could, my peers would jump at the chance to work with me. Now was their chance.

I reached out to Dina and made sure Fred was on schedule to start trolling for me come the beginning of the year which was six months before his retirement and enough time to make everyone rich, including him, before he disappeared to an island. I looked down at my watch and saw what time it was—*time to get busy!*

Dina reminded me that Fred was taking care of her *dancer friend* and it was my responsibility to take care of her.

"Dina, don't I always?" I asked.

"Yes, you do, Oz. But I just wanted to remind you."

"Great. Now do me a favor. I'm going to be buried in this project the next few months so I need you to make sure all my clients and contacts coming into Dolls are being taken care of."

"Ozzy, don't I always?" she asked.

"Yes, you do. But I just wanted to remind you."

Flying back to the west coast was, of course, not an easy adventure. My little scarlet letter was hit or miss. Sometimes, I breezed through security. Other times, I was held up and questioned for over an hour. This time was easy but I was feeling like dog shit without my coke. Upon arrival, I tried to make myself feel better by renting a large S-Class Mercedes, instead of my usual convertible.

For the first few days, I traveled around San Diego and signed up collection attorneys that Cal had recommended for Operation Nationwide. Then, back to LA to plan my coming-out extravaganza.

My plan was to throw a hotel room party at the convention and invite every big name in the business. They would all be there, so all I had to do was get these wannabe clients from the convention room floor up to my party room. I rented the twenty rooms on the top floor of the hotel where the convention was being held. (Don't even ask how much that cost.) Proximity was essential. It was a simple elevator ride up to my magical kingdom.

The stress of planning such a critical and wild event threw me clear off the wagon. *Wait—what? You're not surprised?* Anyway, when I fall, I fall hard. I did promise myself to get back on the wagon as soon as I got home. I know, all junkies make that same promise on a daily basis. This time, like every single time I said it before, I was totally serious.

Just like the addition of LSD brought rock and roll to whole new level, the addition of cocaine brought my party planning to new level. I am a naturally high-strung animal. However, being sober for a little while added to the amount of coke I bought was akin to putting a yacht battery into the Energizer bunny. Through my west coast contacts, I hired an elite party crew and made my demand list—DJs, security, strippers, servers, caterers, card dealers, ecstasy, nitrous oxide, kegs, spirits, a kilo of coke, pounds of weed, hash, acid, condoms, dildi, and roofies. *Did I miss anything?*

Naturally, I obtained the convention registration list and put together a poster board of who we needed to sign on. Small guys would be ignored. I didn't have time for people who wanted to pay the least and always ended up complaining the most. We were fishing for humpbacks in the deep blue sea.

Each room had an immoral theme. There was a blackjack room, poker room, coke room, ecstasy room, weed room, and, of course, several fuck rooms. If you woke up drunk and didn't know where you were, you might think you were in a *Hangover* sequel.[98] I had one of my bouncers dress as a priest just to make it interesting. One guy exited from a fuck room and yelled, "Where's that fucking priest? I need confession!"

The fuck rooms were obviously the most important, so I spared no expense staffing two dozen, part-time models, part-time escorts, fulltime freaks. Only
98 Believe me, I'd thought of a tiger way before those producers did.

I had the key to the fuck rooms and they were more closely guarded than the Pentagon. We invited most of the players to the event beforehand and for the rest of the targets, I had my hotties on the convention floor, busting out of their blouses, close them by inviting them upstairs for a drink.

We started at happy hour and it got happier each hour. Within a few hours, everyone on my list was at the DRL blowout party. Vendors abandoned their booths to come up. Men abandoned their children in the streets to come in. Hollywood stars made their way in—and yes, stars you know. One bouncer was tasked with riding the elevator the entire night making sure no posers or pikers slipped through the door.

I played my role as host brilliantly. I was the Mr. Roarke of *Fucked-Up Fantasy Island.* Everyone came upstairs with a fantasy, especially after dropping ecstasy and sucking nitrous oxide, and my job was to make them all come true. I treated my VIPs like rock stars. And cock stars. They got to get fucked up however they wanted and fuck whomever they wanted. As much as they wanted.

All work and no play made Ozzy grumpy. On the other hand, all play and no work made Ozzy broke so I had business to discuss with my distinguished guests before I could dive in to the fray. Once I pitched them how I could now get information no one else could get, it was really a no-brainer for them, even for brains chemically-diminished in capacity. All their collection firms had thousands upon thousands of accounts lying around in need of employment information so that they could file a wage garnishment and eventually get paid. I had already arranged a satellite office through Cal in LA to legitimize my expansion and handle all the new business on west coast. I purposefully didn't mention to my new clients how I would get their desired information and they purposefully didn't ask. Almost all signed on for a remarkable $500 per job locate (half for me, and half for Fred the Fed). Then I dove in and let loose like I just got out of prison.

It cost me $200,000 to make every businessman and lawyer (and even a few celebrities) who came to my party feel what it was like to be me, even if it was just for one night. When the smoke cleared and I had snorted the last line of cocaine, I had more than 30 contracts signed and ready to go. Big contracts for big money. My career at that moment was at its pinnacle of promise. When morning came and it was time to go to bed, I opened up a closet door, walked in, and banged my head on the clothes bar.

I then dropped to the floor, having overdosed on cocaine.

It was now official. I was killing myself with cocaine.

TWENTY TWO

WORD OF MY OVERDOSE GOT BACK TO MY FAMILY IN NEW JERSEY. They plotted an intervention[99] to be carried out as soon as I got back home. Of course, I knew something was coming from them so I intentionally limited my contact with my mother and brother. They were always acting like a couple of DEA agents since I was a kid really, investigating my every move, gathering information, comparing notes, and manipulating my friends. I was also aware that my old lawyer buddy Mikey was playing the role of spy for my family and helping them "act in my best interest." I can't blame him or any of them now, but I shut him out totally at that time. To me, it was a time to accelerate, not brake. Acceleration, I decided, was in my best fucking interest. Acceleration is what my business demanded from me and that is what cocaine demanded of me. This was the most important time of my life, for Crissakes. I had no time to deal with distractions from anyone. I will have time soon enough to get clean. Just not fucking now. Soon. *Sound familiar?* It was

---

99 This wasn't the first time and may not be their last.

starting to sound familiar to me. Like every druggie in history, I told everyone who cared about me that I was fine and to just leave me alone. If they didn't, I shut them out completely.

When I arrived back home, I was in party-hard mode to celebrate surviving my west coast overdose. The night of my welcome home party at my condo, Marty, one of my best buddies going back to our JDR days, never made it over. He was one of my most trusted business associates and had literally bailed me out of a hundred jams over the years. A party wasn't a party without Marty and Marty never missed a party so I must've called him five times that night telling him to get his fat fucking ass over to the condo. He never picked up the phone. Fucking voicemail answered all night.

The next morning, his wife called me. I was still in a coked-up daze when she told me Marty died on his way over. I dropped the phone and down to my knees and cried like my aunts did at their husbands' funerals. Writing about Marty's death makes me cry about it again.

The what-ifs haunted me for weeks. They still do sometimes. *What if I was with Marty like so many other times he was drunk and driving? What if I sent him my car as I often did?* His casket was closed because his death was gruesome. Marty was traveling down Route 80 on his way to my condo and rear-ended a tractor-trailer that was only traveling five miles per hour at the time of Marty's impact. Marty hit the truck with such force that he knocked the tandem wheels completely off the truck and he was decapitated on impact. The police had to remove Marty's head from the back seat of his car. This is what the newspapers mean when they state in an article that a person "died instantly." I had enough contacts in the state police department to learn Marty's blood alcohol level was "in the threes" at the time of the accident.

I was so drugged up that I didn't even make it to the funeral. Everyone there that knew me, I'm certain, thought I was next. Most of them probably thought I would and should have been dead first. In the end, Marty's death was another blaringly loud wake-up call that I completely ignored. And I asked cocaine to help me get through the pain.

◆ ◼ ◆

I ran and ran some more, but could not hide forever from my family's concern. My business pressure was off the charts. I would go for days on end without any sleep, sometimes three or four. Then I would sleep for two days straight and get up and start the madness all over again. It was more like a pathway to suicide than business prosperity. The holiday season was setting in and I was scheduled to launch Operation Nationwide once the calendar turned over to January. After months of prodding me to go into a rehab program, my family and friends finally "surprised" me with a forced intervention. *Interventions always come at the absolute worst times for junkies!*

The problem my concerned loved ones had was, unless I checked myself in voluntarily, they could not compel me to go into a program. Oddly enough, the law was totally on my side. I was a drug addict, but an adult one who was not insane (legally), so no one could tell me what to do. Except a judge.

My loved ones—who I hated at that moment—went around the room and each of them made an excellent case, I must admit now. My mother told me how I wasn't her son anymore. That one hit me the hardest. The hardest at that time and that one actually still hurts when I think about it now. Others pointed out all the tragic aspects and ironies of my life that I was consciously ignoring. I was a multimillionaire yet everyone who cared about me was suffering needlessly watching me lose the battle against the horrible, debilitating disease of addiction. I was a great guy in my own eyes, yet all my ex-girlfriends hated me for hurting them. My real friends were not around anymore, unless they were addicts. This was a problem my money could not solve, nor could I solve it with my bag of tricks. Ultimately, I could not talk myself clean—believe me, I tried that. I was headed to prison or to the cemetery. They knew it. I knew it. It took two gut-wrenching hours, gallons of tears, including some of my own, before I finally relented. I agreed to check in to Bergen Pines, a rehab center located only five miles from my home.

I checked in less than an hour later. After they all left, I checked myself out within minutes. I probably made it home before some of them did. I was not intentionally scamming them and did not want to hurt them any more. I convinced myself I would get clean, but now was just not the time. I explained to my enraged brother that right after the new year, I would go into a fulltime rehab facility in Sussex County. My registration was completed and my date of arrival was scheduled on January 2nd. *Now everyone get off of my fucking back and let me focus on business, please! And getting high.*

To further show my absolute commitment to sobriety, I even agreed to do an outpatient program until I went into the full-time one. Of course this was my strategy to throw them off my scent. As promised, however, I did do the outpatient thing. But right after my sessions, I would go out and get high and drunk with my counselor who was now on my payroll and sympathetic to my situation. My counselor was even sending my family biweekly reports about my "excellent progress." To be fair, I did cut down my daily cocaine use from enough to kill a horse to only enough to slip a pony into a coma. It all worked out swimmingly. My family actually believed I was doing well.

And then came New Year's Eve.

My lawyer friend Mikey knew enough about me and enough people around me to know my commitment to recovery was just another Ozzy front.

Somehow, someway (extreme drug addicts don't recall how things happened on most of their nights), I ended up in a seedy motel on Route 46 in Totowa, New Jersey, with seedy people on New Year's Eve. Mikey knew it. He also knew this was not an unusual event for me. Many nights—too many nights—seemed to follow the same script. A couple years before, Mikey had to send someone to pick me up when I was lying face down in the gutters of Paterson. Try doing that and surviving. Frankly, it may sound hard to believe that I let myself crash so low, but truly, I was no different than anyone else who wrestles with hardcore addiction. Cocaine calls to you like a damsel in distress. And her worshippers will come together and move mountains to answer her call.

In my heyday, I was the most popular abuser in all of northern New Jersey. Everyone called Ozzy to join them for worship at the powdery altar. Not because Ozzy was funny or charming. It was because Ozzy brought an unlimited supply. Getting high was always on Ozzy so getting high was always with Ozzy. In this aspect, Ozzy, the master scam artist, was the ultimate sucker himself.[100]

But that New Year's Eve, Mikey sent in the big guns and they were not there to bring me home. On that night, I woke up with police lights in my bloodshot eyes and guns pointed at my bloated face. My brother was standing right there with them as they busted me on possession and a bunch of other charges. Jail, Mikey thought, was the only way to get me straight.

Off I went. I spent the night in jail vowing to never speak to Mikey or my brother again. That's what drug addicts do when you get between them and their supply.

But all in all, no big deal. A minor bump in the road, really. I was busted on a lot of charges over the years and this one didn't stick either. My brother

100   Yes, I knew it then. But I didn't care.

and Mikey thought they finally had me cornered this time, but I had enough connections to get a suspended sentence "pending my participation in an inpatient rehab program." The only problem was that it was three hours away in a town that should have been named Deliverance, Pennsylvania. Anyway, I went into the court-mandated program for a few days and then picked a fight with the right wrong person and got myself tossed out. Everyone thought I would have to pay the piper once I was thrown out but my *influence*[101] went deeper than Mikey's connections so the law never really caught up to me again when it came to my drug crimes.

Mikey was done with me.

My brother was done with me.

I was glad to be done with them.

However, the law was definitely not done with me and soon found other ways to catch me. Big time.

✦ ✖ ✦

Dina called. Fred was ready for the test, or more aptly stated, the final exam. The list I had organized over the past few months was added to a sizable upfront payment and passed over to him through our female intermediaries. I must say I had the best looking set of cronies of any criminal in history.

Once I got back Fred's hits, I was planning to take them to California and personally teach my west coast crew how to verify and bill them out properly. The west coast was my future because there were no watchful eyes getting in the way of my perfectly functioning addiction, which is what I referred to it as. My east coast operations were still the backbone of my business, hence cash flow, and they were doing remarkably well considering I had not focused on it for months. At this point, the credit must go to my loyal team of employees. Granted, many of them were addicts also, but all of them by now had mortgages to pay and kids to feed so they kept the money train on its tracks even without me. DRL was still getting 10,000 hits per month. My database contained 15% of the entire population of New Jersey in it and it was growing like a fungus. *Boy, those New Jersey boys do sure love to tan, borrow, and not repay.*

Fortunately, my collection clients remained happy in my absence. Hell, maybe they were even happier not to deal with me directly. My insiders at the banks were operating like a smooth criminal spy ring. Our debt buying was growing as we were buying more and more debt as it became available. To keep

101 By *influence*, I mean payoffs and blackmail.

up with tradition, I spread *piece and love* around so people focused on their jobs and stopped worrying about the inevitable crash landing of their boss.

A few weeks later, Dina called again. The *hit list* was in! As soon as I got it, I got on the first flight to LA. Every time I landed in LA, I found myself missing Lily and thought of calling her. Now I didn't say *love*, I said *missed*.

And before you could sing *cha-ching!*, my office crew in California began pumping out the hits like a Top 40 radio station. Our ecstatic clients paid our enormous invoices as soon as they got them. Of course, you did not want to ignore paying the bill from the most lethal collector in the world.

It was a massive undertaking, a boiler room pumping out information and counting the money. As the information went out, the client calls came pouring in. New and existing clients were calling me at all hours of the night begging for me to take on more of their work. I desperately wanted to but there was one problem, Fred was a one-trick pony.

Or so I thought.

Dina called again. I had just landed from California so I told her to meet me in the parking lot of Satin Dolls. When I arrived, she handed me a note that read: "Retirement postponed until the end of the summer. Testing resumes." Fred's words brought tears to my eyes. They were so beautifully and eloquently written. Operation Nationwide was officially extended. I called my Cali-crew and extended their terms accordingly. Like wildfire, word spread far and wide from California to the New York islands, from the redwood forests to the Gulfstream waters... If it sounds like I was singing, that's 'cause I was. And dancing, too, like no one was watching. The work came flooding in instantly like a broken dam. I looked down at my watch and realized what time it was: *it was party time.* So I threw a bash at Satin Dolls to celebrate.

TWENTY THREE

L ABOR DAY IS THE MOST DEPRESSING DAY OF THE YEAR TO A LOT OF PEOPLE, especially people from New Jersey. It signifies the end of the Jersey shore season and the last chance for the illiterate, fake-tan guidos to pump their fists at the beach clubs. Labor Day that year signified the end of an era for me. Fred the Fed officially retired. The deepest information mole I ever had was officially stepping down. No insider connection or infiltration would ever come close to duplicating the value of my run with Fred. It brought me great pride to know that Fred was now "fuck you rich" and I knew he had big plans. He went off to Europe for a month vacation and then on to what I can only describe as a well-deserved Central American sex tour.

Shortly after Fred's retirement, the final payments for Operation Nationwide came in. It was time to square up with everyone, including Dina. All told, we brought in over $11,000,000 billing for Fred's hits. Fred and I together paved the first illegal information super highway. *Beat that Al Gore!* I will always look back fondly and cherish our corrupt partnership. We proved to politicians everywhere that a public-private sector partnership is the most effective business model in this country.

Before he left for vacation, Fred sent word to me that he wished he would have met me ten years ago. I sent word back that if he had, he would have retired nine years ago. Fred made about five million in cash in eight months and it was time for him to go shopping. For an island. I never saw him or spoke to him again. But I will always love him.

I also owed Dina almost a million dollars and I wish today that I would have paid her two million to walk out of my life forever right then and there. She would have definitely taken it, and we'd all be better off today. But instead, I made the mistake of paying her last installment in my limo and stupidly telling her how great of a team we were and how we had accomplished things I never dreamed of. The mistake wasn't actually telling her that because that was true. The mistake was convincing her to finally celebrate with me with a little champagne and coke. The drugs and alcohol soon led to the tears about how her married boyfriend just broke up with her. Immediately, I thought to myself, "This is not good!"

Then Little Ozzy looked up at me and said, "What the fuck are you talking about? This is fuckin' awesome!" The coke and Little Ozzy overruled Big Ozzy's better judgment. Obi-Wan Kenobi was wrong. The Dark Side is far more powerful. Looking back, I did what every man would with a bombshell stripper crying in his limo—played the sympathy card by telling her how beautiful, smart, and rich she was.

Not to brag, but it is important for me to point out I must have fucked well over a thousand girls in my day (and painfully none for a while now). But I was not your typical swinging cocksman. I don't remember half of them and I paid for most of them, one way or another. (but don't we all?) I had no rules, no standards, and zero shame. I was a sex-addicted freak. But somehow, deep in the back of my coke-clouded mind, I knew that this one—this beautiful, vulnerable, woman ripe for the easy picking after so much trying—was the only one I should have passed on in my entire life.

Before I knew it, Dina was my girlfriend. Ain't that the way it happens for all men? My mother was thrilled with the news because she'd begged me to settle down and marry my girlfriends my whole adult life. Didn't she know that women ruined everything great in this world? Just look at The Beatles.

Still, my mother believed a wife and family would be the only way I would get clean. Perhaps she was right. Dina was someone she really pushed for. She was a stripper but, then again, most of them were. The difference was Dina was Italian. And that meant she was perfect.

"Ozzy, why-a you-a no-a want to-a marry-a Dina?"

"Are you insane, Mom?"

"No-a! I-a think-a that-a you-a should-a marry-a dis-a girl."

"I don't even like her," I yelled.

"Then-a why-a you-a move-a in-a with-a her?"

"I WAS HIGH!" I shouted and hung up.

It was true. I was high. *I know, I know, I was always high.* But during those final days, I was my highest. I'd had relationships before. Some of them even with good religious girls who waited until they were married until they slept with me. Almost all of my girlfriends tried to tame me, even the wild ones. None of them could. An exorcism conducted by the Pope and a flock of Cardinals (or seagulls) couldn't repel my demons. Most of my women were of the fly-by-night variety and I was perfectly fine with that. I always said that women were the only people I never lied to... after sex.

A former girlfriend said it best when she told me once that I was a great place to visit but she wouldn't want to live there. Some were not, let's say, as "easy go" as they were "easy come." Like you would expect along the scorched earth of my past relationships, there were entrapping pregnancies, forced abortions, payoffs, threats, and blackmailing. The kind of female company I kept, and the kind of guy I was, required me to utilize my unique set of skills and connections to chase many woman away. That was just the cost of being Ozzy.

The reality was Dina moved in because I believed it was a wise business move for me. After all, she was raking in money from me so that is how I convinced myself. I would cut down on labor expenses. And, truth be told, the sex was mind-blowing. Of course, no one on planet earth who knew me expected it to last long. Except Dina.

I bought two adjacent condos so I could have more space. I used one as a personal office and we lived together in the other. Now don't go off imagining bowling night and dance recitals. It's not like I gave up my rock star lifestyle for Dina. It was more like she joined the band as my number one groupie.

Dina was a doll and did not discriminate against women, so she would routinely come home with friends for a threesome. Then I started having threesomes with just her friends. It was a wild ride for a while, but just like everything else I touched, it got madly out of control. Someone once said to me: you can't have the crazy in bed and the calm out of it. Someone *should* have said to me: jealousy, cash, and cocaine do not mix well together.

Before we hooked up, I treated Dina with the utmost respect. She was my best and most trusted representative for years. My clients loved her. She knew how to keep them happy with the ladies. Without her, there would have been no Fred. She made a fortune. I made a fortune.

After she moved in, Dina stopped being concerned about her job and making money and started being concerned only about marrying me to spend mine. I started to treat Dina like a whore because she stopped being valuable to me. It was my fault. This is why they say don't mix business with pleasure: it always turns into mixing business with misery.

You may think it's been dark and ugly since page one, but this is the part where it starts getting really dark and ugly from my perspective. Like never before, I buried my nose in coke and battled it out with Dina. I felt trapped. Really trapped. I couldn't just toss her out with the trash like I could with other "girlfriends" so I tried to force her to leave by her own volition. I was a professional partier so I stayed away for days. Didn't call. Didn't answer. Unplugged and disconnected from our relationship. Each time, Dina would somehow plug me back in. Rather than leave me, she followed me. She spied for and plotted with my family and became obsessed with trying to get me sober. Like William fucking Wallace, I vowed *RESISTANCE!* When she demanded that I quit drinking and drugging, I yelled, "I'm not a fucking quitter!"

The plan she ultimately concocted with my mother was—ready for this—to marry me! I couldn't believe it. The way that I looked at it was why would I marry a woman with such low standards in a man? I told her and my mother, "No fucking way. Never."

Then Dina put another diabolical plan together with her close friend Kathy: get me busted again and into rehab. They figured I would then sober up, come to my senses, realize I really loved her, and we would live happily ever after bowling with her boring fucking friends in the suburbs.

✦ ◼ ✦

One night, I came home and Dina's friend Kathy was there having dinner. Dina asked me if I had any coke because Kathy and her were in need. I checked and I was all out, which was strange as I could have sworn I had some left. Anyway, I went out to pick up a package of white dynamite. The evening had threesome written all over it. *Did I mention how freaky the sex with Dina was?* Plus, Kathy was an excellent third wheel and I do love riding a tricycle!

Anyway, while on my way to my pharmacist (who worked only the night shift on dark corners), a call came in from a friend of mine who was a Hackensack cop. He tipped me off that dispatch received a call from a Bergen County narcotics officer who was planning on doing a motor vehicle stop on one Orazio Lembo of Prospect Avenue and he needed back up.

I looked at my watch saw what time it was: It's go time. Go to hell time. I hung up and pulled into a self-serve car wash and vacuumed my car twice to eliminate any dust from residual illegal substances. I then went to the White Castle drive-thru and bought burgers. As I was turning into my condo parking lot, the lights and sirens blared. The cops cut me off and swarmed me like I was Orazio Bin Laden. Their guns were out as they told me to exit the vehicle. *Busted!* Or was I?

Detective Eric Hochman, the asshole in charge, shoved me against the hood, started patting me down and barked, "Where you coming from?"

"Your mother's house," I confessed. I noticed some of the other cops smirking. I guess they all knew Eric was an asshole.

Eric then searched me. Nothing. I could see him starting to sweat like a stripper at a spelling bee. He searched my vehicle everywhere. Nothing. He sweated some more. He even opened the case to my sunglasses—to which I shouted out, "You found it! There's a kilo in there, Detective!"

I happily consented to a trunk search before he even asked to embarrass him some more. It was a treat to see his face when he opened it and saw all the fresh vacuum streaks. Now he was enraged. I kept telling him to hurry up as his mother would be worrying as to where I was. He told me to shut the fuck up. I responded by telling him I won't consent to an anal cavity search no matter how much he begged me.

I would have been a dick to any cop in that scenario, but Eric was a different scenario than meets the eye. You see, we knew each other. Eric was in love with Dina and jealous of everything I was about. He hated me and hated my life. He wanted me locked up in the worst way so he could save Dina and have her to himself. That was how he would win. Dina hypnotized him with her tit bombs to get him to lock me up so she and I could get married. He, on the other hand, wanted to lock me up so he could marry her. *What a fucking misfit soap opera.*

I hated all cops who were not on my payroll. And they hated me. We were natural born enemies. Eric was the worst kind of cop, a loser who used his badge to be tough and get in women's pants.

Ashamed, Eric eventually had to give up. There was nothing to be found. I could tell some of his peers enjoyed watching his embarrassment.

To comfort him and hopefully alleviate some of his embarrassment in front of his fellow officers, I told him, "That was some outstanding detective work, fuckface," and walked into my building with my burgers.

I had totally fucking won this battle, but we both knew it was far from over.

The co-conspirators upstairs were visibly shocked to see me. It was crystal-clear to me that they took my stash and set me up. But I played dumb for now. I dropped the burgers on the table with a casual smile on my face and then pretended to go wash up. Instead, I went into my closet and took out my FM transmitter and portable scanner. I put the scanner in my coat pocket and placed the transmitter in a plant by the kitchen. Just to rub it in, I told the girls I forgot the coke in the car and I was running down to get it. I walked out of the condo, down one flight of stairs, and tuned in to my desired frequency. I immediately heard them questioning each other about what could have happened. Dina then told Kathy to go into the bathroom and call Eric to find out. That was all I needed to hear.

Within an hour, I had my runners come over with a van to pack me up. Dina was *shocked* and played the dumb routine, which I had invented back in 1994. She wouldn't leave me, so I was leaving her. We both knew what she had tried to do to me. It failed. Now it was my turn. Betrayal is a son of a bitch, especially when it fails.

"What am I supposed to do about bills and money?" she yelled while my guys started moving me out.

I reached into our nightstand, grabbed a giant dildo, handed it to her, and said calmly, "Go fuck yourself."

✦ ✖ ✦

After my bust of her bust, she changed her tune to concerned girlfriend who was trying her own version of forced intervention. My mother was hired as her defense lawyer. When that failed, she resorted to threatening me that she was going to the police unless I paid her 50 grand. Many people, including strippers, tried extorting me in the past. They all had little credibility and limited knowledge, so it was easy to swat them down, one way or another. Dina was different. She had information that no one else knew. And she was a woman possessed.

So yes, I was concerned. And no doubt, that asshole Eric was frothing at the mouth to finally bust me after his spectacular failure earlier and I know Dina was leaning her saline-filled tits on him to keep him focused on the bullseye, which was my ass in the slammer. She was also used to spending like a lottery winner and now she was eliminated from my business and off the gravy train. That meant *back to the pole!* Because I was still fucking half the girls at Satin Dolls, they kept me informed about Eric being in there all the time talking to Dina. I knew everything they were up to.

I had runners on Dina 24/7. They tailed her every move. I tapped all my law enforcement contacts and paid them more to keep their ears opened wider and longer about me. The cocaine was a driving force of revenge and paranoia. I watched my security cameras all day like it was a great movie. I was watching the cops who were watching me. I was calling the cops who were watching the cops who were watching me. I was getting inside information, reports from moles. It was a game of cat and mouse. I had my friends get my coke and stash it with them. I was too hot to keep it on or near me. I considered *all options* to get her and Eric off my back.[102]

Then there were the times I considered suicide. I think all long-term, hardcore drug addicts consider this regularly.[103] I just wanted to wake up sober from the night before. I did not want the pain I was putting myself through anymore. I wanted the nightmare I'd created to end. Some way. Any way. I thought about going up to the roof of my building and jumping off. Then I realized I wouldn't even jump off a curb, never mind a ten-story drop.

Why didn't I just pay Dina? Because that bitch burned me. Looking back— *oh, that prisoner hindsight*—it would have been wise to simply pay her off and videotape it all to blow up her credibility against me. But I was not about to bend over for anyone, let alone some bitch stripper trying to shake me down. And at this point, any sense of reason had blown away like dust in the wind…

102 I'll leave it to you, dear reader, to decide what *all options* entails.
103 Funny how we never consider rehab.

or coke up my nose.

But Dina was also feeling the heat. She was drinking heavily and one night fell off the Satin Dolls stage. A patron laughed at her and she threw a shot glass at him but hit another girl sitting with a customer. That was it. The owner fired her on the spot. She was spiraling out of control and she blamed me. *Of course!*

The next morning, I learned she was in the hospital for trying to kill herself. I felt no sympathy. It was her fault for fucking with me in the first place. To drive it home, I sent her one last reminder by sending her a dozen long-stem red roses in a vase with a note attached that read: *Better luck next time.* I didn't sign it, but I didn't have to. Then…

Knock! Knock!

And the party ended.

TWENTY FOUR

FEBRUARY 9, 2005 WAS A GLORIOUS DAY FOR MY NEMESIS ERIC. ME, NOT SO MUCH. He came to my door with an older colleague and a search warrant. The older detective asked, "Did you know we were coming?" I was satellite high and sloppy drunk, so I grabbed a hold of his jacket and yelled, "I've been waiting for you fucking guys for ten fucking years!"

Being the best unknown actor in the world, I then nosed-dived right down to the floor and improvised a fake seizure, including the foam and convulsions. They reluctantly rushed me to the hospital in an ambulance—better than jail for the time being—and by the time the cops were able to talk to me, my attorney was already there to stop them. My mother showed up, saw my leg cuffed to the bed, and started to break down, but I threw her a wink and she winked back, proud of her son, Al "Ozzy" Pacino.

However, my award-worthy theatrics did not impede their search. Although they didn't find everything, they found enough. What broke my case was that my company was doing a collection for Uncle Louie's friend who owned an escort service. The owner of the escort service had extended credit to a client for coke and women and when the client disappeared without paying, DRL was hired to locate the client. We tracked him down and located his place of employment. Soon thereafter—and *totally coincidentally*—the target slipped and fell down three flights of stairs (twice) in the building of the mortgage company where he worked. The in-person collector told him that he would be back tomorrow and that he better have the money. The target did not want to slip anymore and cut a check out of his boss's account. Not knowing the check was stolen, I deposited it into my client trust account as I had to keep everything legit. The check was returned by the bank as "refer to maker" because the owner of the company had reported it stolen. Since the mortgage company was in Hackensack, and so was DRL, the check conveniently landed right on the desk of that asshole Eric, the fuckface detective. With the stolen check placed in my account and with Dina's statement, it was finally enough for a judge to issue a search warrant for my office. *Ain't that a bitch?*

I bailed out on $250,000 bond and immediately checked myself into rehab at the recommendation of my criminal attorney. The police confiscated everything from my dirty underwear to my shore house, and most notably, all thirteen computers in my office. I completed a 28-day program and then did another one. *That's right—back-to-back rehabs baby!*

On April 28, 2005, as soon as I checked out of my second rehab stint, the cops came to my mother's house and arrested me again. The indictment was thick as a brick, a total of 54 fucking counts including, but unfortunately not limited to: first-degree racketeering, first-degree money laundering, and "masterminding the largest breach of bank security in American history."

On the car ride to the police station, the cops tried to break me. I told them they should read my indictment before they tried their Jedi mind tricks. One told me that if I was convicted on these charges, I was facing 130 years in prison and a 1.5 million dollar fine. I leaned my head into the front seat and responded, "Yeah. And what are you going to do to me if I don't pay the fine? Give me another hundred years?" The rest of the ride was quiet.

My arrest made international news. It was that day that the banking industry's worst fears were realized. One thing I am grateful to the media for is they saved me all the time of having to call my clients to tell them I was out of business for the foreseeable future. Beside myself, there were also eight other co-defendants that were charged with me. Not bad considering there were dozens of accomplices over the years. Mikey told me my competitors and/or the people close to my operation who were not charged were likely the rats and that the case against me had clearly been pieced together over years through multiple informants.

Statistics showed that if you owed a debt in New Jersey between 1992 and 2005, there was an 80% chance that I was somehow, someway associated to your claim. So what did the banks do about that? They went into damage control mode and minimized the number of accounts that were breached down to a few hundred. *Now how about that?* I robbed these fools blind and they responded by helping my defense. *Thanks guys!* I wonder if their customers, who entrusted these institutions with their life savings, ever found that a wee bit concerning.

Anyway, the US Treasury Department joined the Fuck Ozzy Party and audited everything. It took almost a year before they issued a report of some 60,000 pages, which concluded that over 900,000 accounts were pierced, totaling an estimated 1.6 trillion dollars.

Nice work gentlemen, but you were way off. Why? They basically only had four years of my records. The real numbers…were almost double theirs. But who's counting?

Most interestingly, the report also stated that not one penny was missing nor was anyone's personal identity information compromised. (I wonder if the banks asked for that to be included.) They ended their findings by stating any and all information "taken" was utilized through the court system to legally collect debts. Of the more than 900,000 accounts that were accessed illegally by me, no money was stolen and no one's personal identity had been compromised. Remarkably, all of the accounts that were ultimately levied were done via the courts at an attorney's request. So, as it turned out, I wasn't the problem after all. I was the solution. Like Robin Hood. I took from the wrong (almost legally), and gave to the wronged (legally). *Don't you think I deserve an apology and a thank you for my service to justice?*

I believe my case was the first one in Bergen County history to ever be assigned two prosecutors. When they learned of the contents of the report, they offered me a reduced sentence if I would sign a statement stating that the attorneys who purchased my information knew that it had been obtained illegally. I told them to go fuck themselves. Nicely.

Eventually I copped a deal without ratting. I could not roll the dice on 30 years in prison. On May 11, 2007, in a jam-packed courtroom, I was about to be sentenced and I was high as a kite on coke.[104] The judge first asked no one in particular, "How can one man be solely responsible for the largest breach in bank security in American history?" Not quite the opening line you like to hear when your head is the one on the guillotine.

Before he sentenced me, the judge asked me, "Mr. Lembo, in your case the opportunity to steal money was there, and you never took it. May I ask why?"

"Because that is not the way my mother raised me!" The courtroom, filled with reporters, was silent as they absorbed my response.

The judge then asked me one last question, "Before I impose my sentence on you, is there anything that you would like to say?"

"Yes," I responded. "Did I tell you how handsome you look today, Your Honor?" This time the courtroom erupted in laughter. The judge even smirked. Truth was, he was not particularly handsome.

All of my co-defendants received probation. I was sentenced to five years in state prison and sent down to Bayside State Prison located in Leesburg. After serving seven months, I entered into an early release program known as ISP, which stands for Intensive Supervision Program. They call it *prison without the walls*. It's like a kind of hardcore probation or parole.

But after two years in the ISP program, I was violated for a technicality. Why? Well…ummm…do you really want to know? Okay…okay…I was kind of having sexual relations with my supervising officer. But I didn't get busted for banging her—and really it was more like she was banging me (picture an elephant fucking a flea). Anyway, while it lasted, the benefits this arrangement afforded me were too numerous to list. What happened though was one day, she wasn't the one who showed up to my apartment. Her supervisor showed up and, although he was not interested in sexual relations, he certainly wanted to nail me. *Ain't that another bitch?*

As usual, Mikey had warned me about that, but of course I was getting high again and not listening. The officer came right in and searched my computer and discovered that I was doing credit repair work. Turns out, that was a no-no per my conditions. But Officer, I was using my expertise to help people rehabilitate

---

104 You really didn't think I would remain clean, did you?

their credit so they can establish better ratings, borrow, and get back on the right financial track—meaning I was now negotiating for individuals in their dealings with their collectors. And really, who would be better to represent people against collectors than me? Relatively speaking, it was like stopping a top doctor from caring for sick children. It was not dirty work, but the government did not see it that way. My urine, however, was also dirty, which was also a no-no per my conditions.

I was officially violated and sent to Jones Farm, a minimum security correctional facility located in Trenton. They called it prison, but I've been to preschools that were tougher than this place. While doing my time, I was playing basketball one day and banged my shoulder into the wall. It seemed that a mole that was growing had started to bleed and would not stop. I asked the doctor to take a look at it and he did. He decided to remove the mole and told me that it looked like a blood blister but he would do a biopsy anyway. Little did he or I know, he saved my life...for the time being.

About a week later, he called me back in, sat me down, and told me it was cancerous. He also told me if the cancer has already spread to my brain or bones that I would have between six months to two years to live.

That silenced me. I didn't know what to say or what to feel. I walked out saying nothing. I was lost, all alone in prison, and I could be dying. I remember walking over to my bunk and burying my face in a pillow and crying my eyes out. Prison is the worst environment imaginable to expose yourself at your weakest and most vulnerable. *Would I ever get the chance to live a life free of crime, free of punishment, free of drugs?* If I was outside of prison, I have no doubt I would have overdosed again or been found face down on some mean street within 48 hours or both.

My physical body was drug-free, but mentally I was not sober long enough nor was I strong enough to handle being dealt a hand of potential terminal illness. If I had access to drugs, which I did not, I would have turned to them for the strength to get me through it. My brother and Mikey were right. Prison actually saved my life. In more ways than one.

It took awhile, but eventually I stopped crying about it. I remembered that my attitude was always the core factor in my life. From that day on, I vouched to not fear cancer. Cancer would now fear me.

I take great solace knowing I'm alive and soon will be out of prison. Then, I hope to be my mother's son again.

As for you, I can only hope you never get bullshitted by someone like me. Again.

EPILOGUE

At the young age of 41, Orazio "Ozzy" Lembo, Jr. died unexpectedly too old. Although neglected skin cancer is a swift, lethal killer, it is nevertheless categorized under natural causes. And a natural cause was the least expected demise for a life of addiction, overdoses, jealous boyfriends, betrayed girlfriends, crime, prison, drug dealers, intoxicated driving, wiseguys, dumb guys, pimps, and prostitutes. Ozzy Lembo cheated death dozens of times. He survived thousands of bad decisions made late at night with bad people in bad neighborhoods. Every time he woke up from a blurry, blacked-out toxic binge, Ozzy had further proof of his own invincibility to go with his hangover. He even beat skin cancer once before. And for those reasons he believed he was immortal. That belief did not cause his skin cancer to return, but it made him ignore it...until it was too late.

Ozzy professed to be a modern day Robin Hood, a heroic outlaw advancing a noble cause. Who could argue that uncovering deadbeat debtors' intentionally hidden assets so lawful creditors could collect what they were rightfully entitled to was not a just quest? If you disagree, then you are probably lucky enough to never have been owed money from a deadbeat hiding their assets from you. Or perhaps you are presently hiding your assets from your creditors, possibly your ex-wife—in which case after reading this book you will find great comfort in learning Ozzy is no longer alive to catch you.

Just like his legendary predecessor from the Sherwood Forest, Ozzy donated all his criminal spoils to his favorite charity. In Ozzy's case, it was his personal life of mayhem and excess. He earned millions righting injustices and blew all of it, much of it right up his nose. He did not carry a bow and arrow and never drew a sword to steal what he was after. Ozzy robbed completely unarmed in the middle of the day without anyone noticing he was doing it. He perfected and deployed the most powerful weapon of all—one that has separated more people from their money than any other in history—bullshit. Sure, he masterminded a combination of technology, aliases, sex, payoffs, moles, and bribes to commit the largest breach of security in US banking history, but it was his fearless and brilliant capacity to bullshit that made Ozzy Lembo a criminal genius like no other.

Ozzy was a criminal ghost. A friendly ghost, you could say. Invisible to the most sophisticated security measures. Invisible to his unsuspecting prey. His victims never sensed a predator was lurking. They never met him. They never interacted with him, except if he was posing as someone else. They never even knew that a crime was how their hidden personal financial information was uncovered. After all, so many of them were hiding dishonestly themselves. That is why Ozzy was able to be so successful at his craft for so long. He created a veil between him and his not-so-innocent victims that insulated him from their detection. He operated as a criminal wizard behind an impenetrable curtain of deceit. A bad guy catching bad guys. That was the wizardry of Ozzy. To this day, years after his bust, most of his victims do not realize they actually were his victims. You may know someone who was his victim. If you lived in New Jersey during the 90s, then you likely knew one of his victims. You may have been his victim. Heck, I may have been his victim. And, if not for the typical line of rats and enemies that a drug-infused, non-stop-party lifestyle breeds, law enforcement may never have thought to peek behind the curtain and arrest the wizard.

As you would expect, once they were informed about Ozzy's operation, the government went after him like any other robbing hood. Ozzy's arrogance, always on full display, especially to authorities, made them all the more determined to put a stop to the non-stop party and bring him down. To the government, Ozzy was a low-life junkie that lived the high life by breaking the law. Fittingly, when they did finally catch him, they threw an encyclopedia of charges at him that threatened to bury him in a prison cell for the rest of his life.

So how did he end up with a relative slap on the wrist in prison time? At the time, people logically assumed he did what everyone else whose liberty is threatened does for leniency—rat out those above and around him in exchange for a lighter sentence. Despite what he told you in the preceding pages, Ozzy was not beyond saving his own ass at the expense of other asses. That option was thoroughly discussed; however, in the end, he had no play. Why? Ozzy sat alone on the tip of his criminal pyramid. He had no equity partners and no equal peers to point the finger at. His network of paid insiders each played a very specific role and none of them knew (or wanted to know) how Ozzy fit them all together. Sure, others—primarily creditors' attorneys—used the information Ozzy stole, but that use was for legitimate reasons: to collect legal debts on behalf of their creditor clients. For these reasons, coupled with his voluble disdain for authority, the government craved Ozzy the Dark Wizard more than anyone else.

Ozzy's criminal case did benefit from a fortuitous set of circumstances he was able to capitalize on. For one, the laws on the books at that time did not foresee, hence, did not specifically criminalize many of his pioneering tactics. As a result, his able criminal counsel was poised to present formidable defenses at trial based upon a number of technicalities. (Remember, prosecutors, much to their chagrin, could not prove the information stolen by Ozzy was used illegally because it wasn't.) Secondly, and perhaps most tellingly, the last thing the country's most powerful banking giants wanted was a bright-light trial on display for their customers to learn firsthand how easily and deeply one man pierced their pathetic privacy safeguards. No bank in the world wanted Ozzy's side of story to be told, including the ones he did not actually penetrate or victimize. Consequently, the government slapped Ozzy as hard as they could have (and should have) under the delicate totality of circumstances.

The media claimed Ozzy's crimes would make "Al Capone blush" and "Dillinger envious." As a result of his innovative schemes, laws and regulations were reviewed and rewritten. Meetings were held in banks to discuss their internal security and employee controls. It must have been impossible for bank executives to wrap their highly-educated heads around how a young man with a high-school education, who was not even computer savvy, outsmarted the banking world for thirteen years right before their very eyes. Master scammers like Ozzy are the reason why you get frustrated dealing with all the hurdles your bank puts in front of you when you are simply trying to access your own financial information. Ozzy is why a teller who knows you for years is still required to check your identification like you are a total stranger. Ozzy is why you cannot get anywhere on the phone with phone companies, cable companies, or the DMV. Ozzy duped them all a thousand times and forced them all to reconsider their protocols. If they haven't done this already, I'm sure they will after reading this story. On the other hand, you also have schemers like Ozzy to thank for fairer debt and collection laws. And if you're a deadbeat debtor, then Ozzy's conviction has been a godsend to your conniving.

When Ozzy got caught violating the terms of his early release program he was more terrified than his ego would ever permit him to admit in retrospect. He was not afraid of facing the dangers of prison again—Ozzy was admired by his felonious peers and even liked by most of his captors. He was terrified because it meant forced sobriety. And forced sobriety is the most frightening reality a hardcore addict ever has to face. Ozzy begged me to represent him and help him overturn his "unfair" violation. Had I agreed, and if his family and certain friends agreed to essentially lie for him, he just may have been able to wiggle out of prison the second time around. We all refused and he resented us for not helping him when, in his mind, we so easily could have. Of course, he refused to admit to me what we all knew was true—that he was coked-up again and prison was his only hope to get clean. As he went back into prison, I urged him to write his memoirs down because it would help him heal and recover.

After Ozzy was released the second and final time, he handed me his memoirs and asked me to complete the story. He had dealt with hundreds of lawyers during his lifetime and always told me he trusted only one. He may have trusted me, respected my advice, and greatly admired my father, but he hated me for plotting his sobriety and rarely listened to me (or any other counselor). But still, Ozzy wanted me to fill in the blanks about his life, his crimes, his case, and other relevant information that he left out or forgot after so many years of cocaine abuse. With thirty years of friendship, fifteen as confidential counsel, I knew things about Ozzy and his crazy life that no one else did. I also knew a lot of things about him that he did not know and he would not want others to know. When I reminded him of this, he told me to write whatever I felt was necessary to tell the whole story.

I purposely delayed our collaboration, but not because I wasn't interested. I had no doubt the world would be blown away by Ozzy's story. After all, there's a lot to learn from one of the best scam artists and bullshitters in history. My hesitation was solely because I also knew that if he were ever to taste success again, this time potentially as a celebrity, Ozzy's demons would immediately seize control. Just like they always had. So I resisted his request to finish what he started...until everything changed.

As you would expect from an unapologetic egomaniac, Ozzy brushed over much of the devastation he caused to his family, his friends, and even himself in this book. You didn't see it in this memoir because he didn't see it in his own life. Ozzy was a tornado of excitement and fun that blew into people's lives at a hundred miles an hour and swept them up in his storm of personality, generosity, and carnality. Eventually he would spit most of them back out, and they were often irreparably damaged from their association with him. This is why most names have been changed. There are many who have suffered enough heartache from the life and death of Ozzy.

Accordingly, I will not permit Ozzy's parents to read this book. I will also continue to strongly discourage his brother from reading it also. Joe Lembo has forged a life diametrically opposite to the one led by his infamous younger brother. Oddly enough, you will not find a more honest and truer family man than Joe Lembo. His younger brother, on the other hand, was the family maniac. Anyone who ever loved Ozzy was hurt badly by him, in many instances intentionally. Ozzy also hurt everyone he loved, especially his brother and parents, and that made him feel guilty. And guilt made him take more drugs. And drugs made him cause more hurt. Some associates who were burned by Ozzy got their revenge, and, as you see, Ozzy went to his grave not even knowing everyone who turned on him in the end.

The last phone conversation I had with Ozzy was when he was on the way to the doctor's office to get checked for another growth on his shoulder. He was talking at typical light-speed about me representing him in the sale of his life story while I expressed my concern about his new growth. He brushed off my concern and told me there was nothing to worry about except what to pack for our business trip to Hollywood. I didn't believe his new growth was nothing, but I knew he believed it. He was broke, but sober, at least by his personal standards, which considered continuous marijuana use guiltless long before the State of Colorado did. The former multimillionaire rockstar collection wizard was living back at his parents' home. No girlfriends orbited him. No luxury cars or stretch limousines waited for him in the driveway. The cash was gone. Blown on coke, lawyers, and otherwise lost because he forgot where he hid it all. There was no evidence remaining of his legendary extravagances. Only foggy distant memories. And now, a growth had returned not long after being previously treated for malignant melanoma in prison. But he was far from depressed. After all, Ozzy Lembo was finally free from the pesky government authorities.

Even with a body fighting stage four cancer, Ozzy's mind was focused on the future. And the future was bright for the dark wizard. He would write his comeback chapter with the same irrepressibility that created a one-of-a-kind, one-man criminal empire. There was no doubt in his mastermind that the world would soon be introduced to the incredible true story of the fake character Ozzy Lembo. A few weeks after we hung up the phone, the wizard was dead, his body overrun with tumors.

Everything changed.

~ *Michael Taromina*

Made in the USA
Middletown, DE
05 September 2015